History &
Theology
in the
Fourth
Gospel

For Dorothy

in whom that name is fulfilled

History&
Theology
in the
Fourth
Gospel

Revised and Enlarged

J. Louis Martyn

ABINGDON
Nashville

HISTORY AND THEOLOGY IN THE FOURTH GOSPEL

Library of Congress Cataloging in Publication Data

MARTYN, JAMES LOUIS, 1925-
History and theology in the Fourth Gospel.
Bibliography: p. 164.
Includes index.
1. Bible. N.T. John—Criticism, interpretation, etc. 2. Bible. N.T.
John—Theology. I. Title.
BS2615.2.M34 1979   226'.5'06   78-10634

ISBN 0-687-17150-4

MANUFACTURED BY THE PARTHENON PRESS AT
NASHVILLE, TENNESSEE, UNITED STATES OF AMERICA

Contents

Part I   A Synagogue-Church Drama:
                                      Erecting the Wall of Separation

Part II   After the Wall Is Erected:
                                                The Drama Continues

Part III   Major Theological Terms
of the Conversation

Abbreviations

1. Books and Articles

Barrett, *St. John*	C. K. Barrett, *The Gospel According to St. John* (1955).
Bauer, *Johannes*	W. Bauer, *Das Johannesevangelium, HNT* (1933³).
Bauer, *Lexicon*	W. Bauer, *A Greek-English Lexicon of the New Testament and Other Early Christian Literature,* trans. and adapted by W. F. Arndt and F. W. Gingrich (1957).
Bernard, *St. John*	J. H. Bernard, *A Critical and Exegetical Commentary on the Gospel According to St. John,* 2 vols., ed. A. H. McNeile (1928).
Billerbeck, *Kommentar*	H. L. Strack and P. Billerbeck, *Kommentar zum Neuen Testament aus Talmud und Midrasch,* 6 vols., vols. 5 and 6 by J. Jeremias and K. Adolph (1922-1961).
Blass, Debrunner, and Funk, *Grammar*	F. Blass and A. Debrunner, *A Greek Grammar of the New Testament and other Early Christian Literature,* trans. and rev. by R. W. Funk (1961).
Bousset and Gressmann, *Religion*	W. Bousset and H. Gressmann, *Die Religion des Judentums* (1926³).
Brown, *John*	R. E. Brown, *The Gospel According to John* (i-xii), *The Anchor Bible,* vols. 29, 29A (1966, 1970).
Bultmann, *History*	R. Bultmann, *History of the Synoptic Tradition,* trans. by John Marsh (1963).

Bultmann, *John*   R. Bultmann, *The Gospel of John* (1971).

Dodd, *Interpretation*   C. H. Dodd, *The Interpretation of the Fourth Gospel* (1954).

Goldin, "The Period of the Talmud"   J. Goldin, "The Period of the Talmud," in vol. 1 of L. Finkelstein (ed.), *The Jews, Their History, Culture, and Religion,* 2 vols. (1949).

Hahn, *Titles*   F. Hahn, *Titles of Jesus in Christology* (1969).

Herford, *Christianity*   R. T. Herford, *Christianity in Talmud and Midrash* (1903).

Hoskyns, *The Fourth Gospel*   E. C. Hoskyns, *The Fourth Gospel,* ed. F. N. Davey (1947²).

Hummel, *Die Auseinandersetzung*   R. Hummel, *Die Auseinandersetzung zwischen Kirche und Judentum im Matthäusevangelium* (1963).

Hunzinger, *Bannpraxis*   C. H. Hunzinger, *Die jüdische Bannpraxis im neutestamentlichen Zeitalter* (Göttingen Dissertation, 1954).

Jastrow, *Dictionary*   M. Jastrow, *A Dictionary of the Targumim, The Talmud Babli and Yerushalmi, and the Midrashic Literature,* 2 vols. (1903).

Jocz, *The Jewish People*   J. Jocz, *The Jewish People and Jesus Christ* (1954²).

de Jonge, *L'Evangile de Jean*   M. de Jonge (ed.), *L'Evangile de Jean, Sources, rédaction, théologie* (1977).

Juster, *Les Juifs*   J. Juster, *Les Juifs dans l'Empire Romain,* 2 vols. (1914).

Käsemann, *Testament*   E. Käsemann, *The Testament of Jesus* (1968).

Klausner, *Jesus*   J. Klausner, *Jesus of Nazareth, His Life, Times, and Teaching* (1925).

Krauss, *Synagogale Alt.*   S. Krauss, *Synagogale Altertümer* (1922).

Abbreviations

Kuhn, *Achtzehngebet*	K. G. Kuhn, *Achtzehngebet und Vaterunser und der Reim* (1950).
Lindars, *John*	B. Lindars, *The Gospel of John* (1972).
Martyn, "Glimpses into the History of the Johannine Community"	J. L. Martyn, "Glimpses into the History of the Johannine Community," in de Jonge, *L'Evangile de Jean,* and in Martyn, *The Gospel of John in Christian History* (1979).
Martyn, "We Have Found Elijah"	J. L. Martyn, "We Have Found Elijah," in R. Hamerton-Kelly and R. Scroggs (eds.), *Jews, Greeks, and Christians, Essays in Honor of W. D. Davies* (1976), and in Martyn, *The Gospel of John in Christian History* (1979).
Meeks, "Man from Heaven"	W. A. Meeks, "The Man from Heaven in Johannine Sectarianism," *JBL* 91 (1972) 44-72.
Meeks, *Prophet-King*	W. A. Meeks, *The Prophet-King, Moses Traditions and the Johannine Christology* (1967).
Moore, *Judaism*	G. F. Moore, *Judaism in the First Centuries of the Christian Era, the Age of the Tannaim,* 3 vols. (1927-1930).
Noack, *Tradition*	B. Noak, *Zur johanneischen Tradition* (1954).
Schnackenburg, *John*	R. Schnackenburg, *The Gospel According to St. John,* vol. 1 (1968).
Schürer, *Jewish People*	E. Schürer, *A History of the Jewish People in the Time of Jesus Christ,* trans. by John Macpherson, 5 vols. (1897-98).
Schulz, *Komposition*	S. Schulz, *Komposition und Herkunft der Johanneischen Reden* (1960).
Schulz, *Menschensohn-*	S. Schulz, *Untersuchungen zur*

Christologie	*Menschensohn-Christologie im Johannesevangelium* (1957).
Tödt, *The Son of Man*	H. E. Tödt, *The Son of Man in the Synoptic Tradition*, trans. by Dorothea M. Barton (1965).
Volz, *Eschatologie*	P. Volz, *Die Eschatologie der jüdischen Gemeinde* (1934²).

2. PERIODICALS, DICTIONARIES, AND OTHER ITEMS
   ABBREVIATED

ATR	*Anglican Theological Review*
b	*Babylonian Talmud*
BAO	*Beihefte zum Alten Orient*
BJRL	*Bulletin of the John Ryland's Library*
CBQ	*Catholic Biblical Quarterly*
CD	*The Cairo Damascus Document*
EvTh	*Evangelische Theologie*
HNT	*Handbuch zum Neuen Testament*
HTR	*Harvard Theological Review*
HUCA	*Hebrew Union College Annual*
IDB	*Interpreter's Dictionary of the Bible*
j	*Jerusalem Talmud*
JBL	*Journal of Biblical Literature*
JEA	*Journal of Egyptian Archaeology*
JQR	*Jewish Quarterly Review*
K-eK	*Kritisch-exegetischer Kommentar über das Neue Testament*
NEB	*New English Bible*
Nov. Test.	*Novum Testamentum*
NTS	*New Testament Studies*
RGG³	*Religion in Geschichte und Gegenwart*, third edition
RSV	*Revised Standard Version*
ThLZ	*Theologische Literaturzeitung*
ThR	*Theologische Rundschau*
ThWNT	*Theologisches Wörterbuch zum Neuen Testament*
ThZ	*Theologische Zeitschrift*
TU	*Texte und Untersuchungen*
USQR	*Union Seminary Quarterly Review*
ZNW	*Zeitschrift für die neutestamentliche Wissenschaft*
ZThK	*Zeitschrift für Theologie und Kirche*

Preface

to First Edition

The origin of the Fourth Gospel is enveloped by mists of unusual density. To achieve a single clearing among them and to realize some of the possibilities of interpretation corresponding to this clearing is the task of the present work.

He who seeks to make a clearing must add to his boldness an adequate measure of humility. The mists conceal surprises. Indeed, they are themselves surprising. They are extensive, so that one necessarily encounters them whatever his avenue of approach. Furthermore, they seem to gather themselves into somewhat independent groups. To dispel the mists on one side is not to conquer those on another. This point demands emphasis because not a few interpreters have mistaken the achievement of a small clearing for a complete removal of the mists. I have had repeatedly to remind myself not to make this same mistake, and I must warn the reader not to do so. The setting in which the Fourth Evangelist composed his work was, I am sure, unusually complex. I have tried to illuminate one aspect of it and to view the interpretative task in light of that aspect.

We have grown somewhat suspicious, I suppose, of the scholar who exclaims that his findings surprise him at least as much as they will surprise any of his readers. I must add to the fund of suspicion. When I began to study the Fourth Gospel, two brilliant articles of Rudolf Bultmann and his incomparable commentary soon convinced me that the conceptual milieu in which the Evangelist penned his work was dominated by a kind of gnostic thought kin to that reflected in the Mandean literature.* The commentary still seems to me an indispensable

---

*"Der religionsgeschichtliche Hintergrund des Prologs zum Johannesevangelium," *Eucharisterion, Festschrift Gunkel* (1923), vol. 2, pp. 3-26; "Die Bedeutung der neuerschlossenen mandäischen und manichäischen Quellen für das Verständnis des Johannesevangeliums," *ZNW*, 24 (1925), pp. 100-46; *Das Evangelium des Johannes, K-eK* (1953[13]).

tool, and its major thesis partly correct. But several remarkable points of correspondence between certain passages in the Fourth Gospel and data from Jewish sources gradually pressed their special claim on me, and I have had to follow a somewhat different path.

The path is different not only with regard to the extra-biblical sources most frequently cited, but also with respect to the way in which the resulting points of correspondence are interpreted. The reader will quickly see that these points of correspondence seem to me not only to illuminate important aspects of the conceptual milieu in which the Fourth Evangelist worked, but also—one might even say primarily—to point toward certain historical developments transpiring in the city in which he lived. It is in the sense thus indicated that I have employed the word history in the title.**

It is pleasant to recall conversations with those who generously read and helpfully criticized the manuscript in whole and in part: colleagues John Knox, Cyril Richardson, and James Smart, friend Ernst Käsemann, former students Robert T. Fortna, Walter Wink, and Ed P. Sanders. Fortna wrote his dissertation (Cambridge University Press)*** on a very important aspect of Johannine studies as I was working at the present task, and the hours we spent together discussing our respective labors were greatly enriching to me. I was also helped by the careful and thoughtful reading of Nils A. Dahl.

The major part of the research and writing was done during a period of scholé made possible by sabbatical leave from Union Theological Seminary and generously sponsored by the John Simon Guggenheim Memorial Foundation. Part of the cost of printing the occasional Greek and Hebrew terms was also graciously borne by the foundation.

J. L. M.
1967

**Contrast, e.g., A. J. B. Higgins, *The Historicity of the Fourth Gospel* (1960).
*** *The Gospel of Signs* (1970).

Preface

to Second Edition

The period since the original edition—almost exactly a decade—has seen the continuation of an extraordinary flow of critical literature on John's Gospel. To make one's way through the major items listed in the bibliographies of E. Malatesta, A. Moda, and H. Thyen† is to see the scope, and indeed, as regards many items, to sense the depth of recent Johannine research. In the midst of such a wealth of publications it is, of course, encouraging to an author to note that certain aspects of his interpretative efforts seem to have borne nourishing fruit. References that are being made to the original edition indicate that its major theses have won a rather wide following.

At the same time, it is no surprise that flaws of some consequence have been detected, and these call for correction. Moreover, some of the most significant items in the bibliographies just mentioned have been directed to issues central to the book, and a revised edition offers a welcome opportunity not only to alter one's line of argument here and there, but also to enter into what one may hope is mutually illuminating conversation with recent interpreters. That conversation will be truly illuminating if it enables us in the midst of our communities to converse more generously with the Evangelist in the midst of his community.

J. L. M.
1978

---

†E. Malatesta, *St. John's Gospel 1920–1965.* A cumulative and classified bibliography of books and periodical literature on the Fourth Gospel (1967); A. Moda, "Quarto Vangelo: 1966–72, Una selezione bibliografica," *Rivista Biblica* 22 (1974), 53-86; H. Thyen, "Aus der Literatur zum Johannesevangelium," *Th R* 39 (1974), 1-69, 222-52, 289-330; 42 (1977), 211-70.

Introduction

Last of all, John, perceiving that the external facts had been made plain in the [other] Gospels, and being urged by his friends and inspired by the Spirit, composed a spiritual Gospel.
—Clement of Alexandria (quoted by Eusebius, *H.E.*, vi, 14, 7)

1. The Problem

More than any other document in the New Testament, the Fourth Gospel has seemed consistently to invite readers in every century to interpret it solely in their own terms. In the Synoptic Gospels, "external facts" are given, and such facts tie those Gospels securely to the time in which they were written. There one encounters a first-century Jew of faraway Palestine, a figure who, however inspiring, stands firmly in his own time and place. He is a Galilean in the original meaning of that term, and while we may listen to many of his words in a direct and simple manner even in our modern age, no reader of the First Three Gospels can fail to sense the many ways in which the synoptic Jesus is far removed from the Western world of today. Like other gifted healers of antiquity, for example, he believes in demons, powers who take up residence in unfortunate persons and who may be exorcised by mighty words.

John's Gospel, on the other hand, seems far more detached from its ancient setting. The very mention of this Gospel causes most of us to think of those marvelous discourses of Jesus, in the reading of which one feels immediately warmed by such "spiritual" and timeless affirmations as, "I am the way, and the truth, and the life." Some of the Johannine Jesus' words seem to be so free of any first-century Palestinian provincialism that we chisel them into the walls of our university libraries, from Chicago to Freiburg, implying that they are philosophical aphorisms, immediately understood in every enlightened age: "You shall know the truth, and the truth shall make you free."

The moderately careful reader discovers, of course, that even this spiritual Gospel has its quite earthy moments. The marvelously general statement above, to take just one example, occurs in the midst of a disquieting, sharp, even unpleasant exchange between Jesus and a group of Jews. For reasons which will certainly take some explaining, Jesus accuses his questioners of trying to murder him, contests their claim to be descended from Abraham, and furthermore suggests that these Jews have as their father neither Abraham nor God, but the devil.

Such discoveries are bound to be disquieting. Yet the source of one's discomfort may be easily enough put aside if one will only be selective in his reading. Within a given chapter—chapter 8, for example, where the saying quoted above is found—one may carefully pick the flowers from among the thorns. Or, considering the Gospel as a whole, one may give most of his attention to the great discourses in chapters 14–16, and, if he has a modicum of mystical sensitivity, he may easily read the "spiritual Gospel" in this way without bothering himself one whit about the world of the first century. Unlike Luther's prophets of ancient Israel, John seems to speak our modern languages with relative ease.[1]

However, for a number of reasons, many persons will refuse the alternative of selective reading, and for them the troublesome elements will remain. To return to the example of chapter 8, why should the Johannine Jesus, himself a Jew, engage in such an intensely hostile exchange with "the Jews"? The question is especially pressing in light of Jesus' clear statement to the Samaritan woman in chapter 4 that "salvation is from the Jews." One is reminded that while some scholars have characterized John's Gospel as the most Jewish of the four, others have argued with equal vigor that it is of all New Testament documents the furthest removed from Judaism.

Such confusion should compel us to look again at the problems

---

[1]Luther's famous remark shows, of course, not only that he was keenly aware of the technical difficulties involved in translating ancient Hebrew texts, but also that he sensed how foreign to his time and place in sixteenth-century Germany were the voices of the Israelite prophets: "How difficult it is to make the ancient prophets speak German!"

Introduction

surrounding the origin of this Gospel. Spiritual—in some sense—it may be. It did not, however, drop from heaven straight into our time, and while we are all willing, no doubt, to agree that it did not, we must go further and energetically seek to define the particular circumstances in response to which this Fourth Gospel was written.

To do so is not to make a journey, of course, into virgin territory. For well over a century scholarly detectives have sifted the evidence and have found no problem in New Testament study more consistently baffling. Furthermore, the question about the circumstances in which the Fourth Evangelist wrote his Gospel is only one of a number of interrelated and highly perplexing problems having to do with the origin of that document.[2] Who was the author? Did he pen also the three Johannine Epistles? In what language did he write the Gospel, and what written sources, if any, did he employ? In what general thought-world did his mind move? Whom did he wish to have as his readers, and what purpose did he have in mind as he wrote for them? Where does his work stand in the history of Christian thought? At what date did he write, and where did he live?

On each of these issues an unusually wide spectrum of opinion, ancient as well as modern, presents itself to the student of Christian origins. One has but to read the summaries of recent work on the Fourth Gospel by Ernst Haenchen, Hartwig Thyen, Robert Kysar, and Rudolf Schnackenburg to see that the "Johannine problem," far from being settled, has grown during the last quarter-century, both in extent and in depth.[3] Relatively few firm conclusions are shared by scholars who have troubled themselves to work with the document itself.

In the present essay we will be concerned in one way or another with several of the questions listed above. Some light on

---

[2]A. Harnack's old saying is still being quoted: "The origin of the Johannine Gospel is . . . the greatest riddle presented to us by the earliest history of Christianity," *Lehrbuch der Dogmengeschichte* (1931), Vol. I, p. 108; cf. van Unnik in *The Gospels Reconsidered* (1960), p. 168.

[3]Ernst Haenchen, "Aus der Literatur zum Johannesevangelium 1929–1956," *Th R*, N.F.23 (1955), pp. 295-335; H. Thyen, "Aus der Literatur zum Johannesevangelium," *Th R 39 (1974), 1-69, 222-52, 289-330; 42 (1977), 211-70;* R. Kysar, *The Fourth Evangelist and His Gospel* (1975); R. Schnackenburg, "Entwicklung und Stand der johanneischen Forchung seit 1955," M. de Jonge (ed.), *L'Evangile de Jean. Sources, rédaction, théologie* (1977), pp. 19-44.

the date of the Gospel may come from the present work, and a few readers may find their ideas regarding its place of origin indirectly confirmed or threatened. We may hope to gain a clearer portrait of at least some of John's prospective readers and, most important of all, a better understanding of his purpose in writing. Our first task, however, is to say something as specific as possible about the actual circumstances in which John wrote his Gospel. How are we to picture daily life in John's church? Have elements of its peculiar daily experiences left their stamp on the Gospel penned by one of its members? May one sense even in its exalted cadences the voice of a Christian theologian who writes *in response to contemporary events and issues* which concern, or should concern, all members of the Christian community in which he lives?

If we should encounter data in the Gospel which indicate an affirmative answer to these questions—and we shall do so very shortly—it becomes imperative that we make every effort to take up temporary residence in the Johannine community. We must see with the eyes and hear with the ears of that community. We must sense at last some of the crises that helped to shape the lives of its members. And we must listen carefully to the kind of conversations in which all of its members found themselves engaged. Only in the midst of this endeavor will we be able to hear the Fourth Evangelist speak *in his own terms,* rather than in words which we moderns merely want to hear from his mouth. And initially it is only in his own terms that he can speak to our time.

2. An Approach to the Problem

How shall we sharpen our senses so as to perceive elements in the Gospel which are clues to the circumstances in which it was written? A word about the role of tradition in early Christian thought may help us find such an approach.

The early church shared with many groups of its time a concern for tradition which exceeds by far that known to most of us. The past—specific events and teachings of the past—lived on with power and somehow mingled with events of the present. To the ancients it was far more obvious than it is to us that one's response to contemporary issues involves careful consideration of the traditions inherited from one's forebears. Indeed it was responsible contemporary involvement which most often sharpened the sense of need for tradition and which is therefore mainly to be thanked for preserving the voice of the past.

Of course not everyone in the early church viewed alike the *relationship* between a concern for tradition and effective involvement in contemporary issues. One of the most pressing needs in New Testament study may be a careful analysis of the various ways in which New Testament authors viewed this relationship.[4] No one will want to insist, I think, that the problem of connecting past tradition with current concerns is viewed in precisely the same way by, say, Paul and Matthew. Yet each has wrestled long and honestly and effectively with just this problem, and a priori there is no reason to doubt that each may have a much-needed word for us as we face the same problem.

One thing, at least, is shared by all New Testament authors in this regard: none of them merely repeats the tradition. Everyone hears it in his own present and that means in his own way; everyone shapes it, bends it, makes selections from among its riches, even adds to it. Put in other terms, everyone reverences the tradition enough to make it his own.

Consequently, when we read the Fourth Gospel, we are listening both to tradition and to a new and unique interpretation of that tradition. With certain reservations, one may compare his experience in this regard with that of listening to Dvořák's *New World Symphony.* There the influence of haunting melodies from Negro spirituals seems unmistakable, and it is obvious that the primitive power of these songs has been felt and honored by the composer. But it is equally obvious that the traditional materials have not been quoted, but rather newly interpreted by the composer for his own time and in response to forces exerted on him in his own milieu. We cannot understand the *New World Symphony* without studying carefully the traditional melodies which Dvořák heard during his American visit, but we must also be at pains to sense the cultural context for which and in which

[4]I have attempted a modest contribution in "Attitudes Ancient and Modern Toward Tradition About Jesus," *USQR* 23 (1968), 129-45, published also in *Student World* 60 (1967), 359-72.

the great European composer interpreted those melodies. Corresponding requirements obtain in the study of John's Gospel.

But now we must proceed carefully. How shall we locate the "traditional melodies" that John received from the past? Were we concerned with Luke, for example, we could assume with probability that we possess a document (Mark) very nearly like one which our author employed. The corresponding assumption is not open to us, I think, when we study the Gospel of John. For good reasons the dominant opinion lies against the view that John used any one of the other Gospels known to us.[5] If we return to our musical comparison, we will need to suppose for the moment that while the traditional spirituals were available to Dvořák, they are known to us only as they stand imbedded in his symphony.

But that is not quite true! While John does not seem to have used the other Gospels known to us, he did after all write a *gospel.* To make the comparison fit, we must actually suppose that several composers have provided us with "new world symphonies," all employing to some degree the same traditional spirituals. One of these composers seems to have worked independently of the others, but he was influenced by some of the same themes.

Thus, by comparing John with the Synoptic Gospels we can

[5]The tide was turned against the theory of dependence by P. Gardner-Smith, *St. John and the Synoptic Gospels* (1938). See also C. H. Dodd, *Historical Tradition in the Fourth Gospel* (1963), and the bibliography in R. E. Brown, *John,* LI. One must also take note of the fact that the thesis that the Fourth Evangelist knew and depended on the Synoptic Gospels is now being vigorously and impressively revived, notably by Frans Neirynck. See his article "John and the Synoptics," pp. 73-106 in M. de Jonge (ed.), *L'Evangile de Jean.* The pertinent questions are also being addressed in a seminar of *Studiorum Novi Testamenti Societas* under Nierynck's direction. Perhaps the consensus which ruled prior to Garner-Smith's work will re-emerge! One can see that it has considerable support in Belgium and Holland; note the article by M. Sabbe, "The Arrest of Jesus in Jn 18, 1-11 and Its Relation to the Synoptic Gospels," M. de Jonge (ed.), *L'Evangile de Jean,* pp. 203-34. Up to the present, however, I have to say that the impressive arguments of Neirynck have not proved convincing to me because the thesis of John's dependence on the Synoptics still seems to create more problems than it solves. For example, if the Johannine church had the Synoptics, it is difficult to understand, as my colleague Raymond Brown has pointed out to me, why the author of the First Epistle of John would not have drawn upon some of their ethical materials in his effort to combat his opponents.

indeed identify many pieces which are obviously traditional: the preaching of John the Baptist, Jesus' own baptism, the calling of disciples, miracles of healing, sharp words of conflict, the triumphal entry into Jerusalem, the cleansing of the Temple, the last supper, the betrayal, the trial, crucifixion, resurrection. Others could be added. On the other hand, it is easy to see that John has handled most of these traditional elements in ways which diverge sharply from those followed by the synoptists. And there are the long discourses, already referred to, which are quite peculiar to John and in which one finds recurring themes not matched in the Synoptics.

Just here a way of approaching our problem emerges. There are in John three miracles of healing: the army officer's son in Capernaum (4:46-54), the lame man at Bethesda in Jerusalem (5:1-9), and the blind beggar near the Temple (9:1-7). All three of these pieces have counterparts in the Synoptic Gospels; they are traditional stories. However, if we read their synoptic parallels and then turn to their use by John, two things strike us immediately: (1) in the case of *the lame man* and *the blind beggar,* John's Gospel shows the miracle story to be the first of a *sequence of scenes.* About this we will have more to say in a moment. Just now it is important to emphasize that by constructing a sequence of scenes based on the miracle story, someone created a *literary genre* quite without counterpart in the body of the Gospels.[6] We may indeed call it a drama. (2) That this "someone" was John himself would seem to be highly probable for reasons that will be presented below. It is just possible, then, that careful attention to *style* and to accents characteristic of the discourses will enable us to distinguish—at least in the stories of the lame man and the blind beggar—between (a) traditional materials and (b) passages in which elements of John's own interests and experiences are more or less clearly reflected.

---

[6]So far as I can see the first productive hint of this fact was given by J. M. Thompson in an article entitled, "An Experiment in Translation," *The Expositor,* Eighth Series, Vol. 16 (1918), pp. 117-25. See also the superb study by Hans Windisch, "Der johanneische Erzählungsstil," *Eucharisterion,* Vol. 2 (1923), pp. 174-213.

Part I

A Synagogue-Church Drama: Erecting the Wall of Separation

1

A Blind Beggar
Receives His Sight

"So he went and washed and came back seeing."

1. Literary Analysis

We begin with John 9 for two reasons. It is a narrative which obviously rests on Christian tradition.[7] And it is constructed in a way that is particularly inviting to the careful reader who wants to distinguish elements that are traditional from those that appear to come from the Fourth Evangelist himself.[8]

a. The miracle story (vv. 1-7).

From a number of similar stories in the Synoptic Gospels and even in other Hellenistic literature, we know about an oral form of tradition which we term a miracle story.[9] The form is naturally somewhat plastic, and we will do well to keep that in mind. Nevertheless we may speak with confidence of three elements which are very often found in the miracle story form.[10]

1. There is a description of the sickness, often emphasizing its serious nature (cf. Mark 2:3).

[7]The Synoptic Gospels offer only two independent stories of Jesus restoring sight to the blind: the narrative about Bartimaeus (Mark 10:46-52, with parallel forms in Matt. 9:27-31, Matt. 20:29-34, and Luke 18:35-43) and a story in which Jesus employs spittle to heal a nameless resident of Bethsaida (Mark 8:22-26). The second of these has the greater number of points in common with John 9:1-7.

[8]It is crucial to note that for the literary analysis pursued at this juncture, and at other key points in the present work, *the basic criteria are provided by the discipline of form criticism.* Thus the major theses that emerge do not depend on any of the current attempts to isolate one or more of the Evangelist's sources. At a few points I have, however, referred to the hypothesis that John employed as one of his sources a Signs Source or Signs Gospel. For bibliography see Excursus E.

[9]In the present discussion, "miracle story" refers to a narrative which relates a miracle of healing, not a nature miracle.

[10]See Bultmann, *History,* pp. 209 ff.; Bultmann, *Form Criticism,* trans. by F. C. Grant (1962), pp. 36 ff.; Vincent Taylor, *The Formation of the Gospel Tradition* (1935'), pp. 121 ff.

24

2. The sick person is healed (cf. Mark 2:11).
3. The miracle is confirmed; the healed person demonstrates his health (cf. Mark 2:12*a*) and/or the onlookers' amazement testifies to the miracle's reality (cf. Mark 2:12*b*).

When we seek to determine the literary form of John 9, we find something quite similar in the opening verses:

1. A description of the malady and an indication that it is hopeless: "a man blind from his birth" (v. 1).
2. The healing itself, with a statement of means and result: "He [Jesus] spat on the ground and made a paste . . . he [the blind man] went and washed and came back seeing" (vv. 6, 7).

Now it is apparent that in verses 8-9 we have something very like the third element, which, while sometimes absent, is often found in such stories: a confirmation of the miracle. Here the reality of the cure is attested by some of the blind man's neighbors; i.e., they account for his sight by explaining that he is not the blind man himself, but rather someone else, perhaps a twin brother who was never blind.

Three important factors, however, point to the inadequacy of treating verses 8-9 in this way. They introduce *as essential characters* persons not previously mentioned, the blind man's neighbors.[11] They clearly begin *a new scene* in which *Jesus is no longer present.*[12] In them one's attention begins to be focused on the formerly blind man, rather than on Jesus. But in the "normal" form of a miracle story, the sick person "comes into view simply as an object of the miraculous cure . . . the interest in him ceases once the miracle has been reported."[13]

That the man's neighbors somehow confirm the miracle may have been the third element in an earlier form of this story. In the

[11]Mark 2:6-10 appears to present a similar phenomenon by introducing the scribes late in the story (contrast Luke 5:17); what we actually have in that case is the combining of an apophthegm with a miracle story. See Bultmann, *History,* pp. 14-16.

[12]Since the miracle story is a means for focusing attention on the healer rather than on the healed person—see especially Bultmann's remarks, *History,* pp. 218 ff.—it is not surprising that Jesus is present throughout the whole of *every* miracle story in the Synoptics.

[13]Bultmann, *History,* pp. 291 f.

present form of the text, however, the neighbors are employed as actors who come onstage only in a separate scene, and who introduce, therefore, what we should probably term *a dramatic expansion* of the original miracle story (vv. 8-41).[14]

b. A dramatic expansion of the miracle story (vv. 8-41).

Three of the major characters in verses 8-41 (two are collective) play no part in verses 1-7: the blind man's neighbors, the Pharisees in council, the blind man's parents. The main accents are also new: that the healing occurred on a sabbath (an afterthought also in 5:10), Jesus' proper identity, synagogue discipline, discipleship to Moses versus discipleship to Jesus, faith in the Son of Man. It scarcely needs further to be argued that verses 8-41 present material which someone composed as an addition to the simple healing narrative of verses 1-7.

Not so apparent is the structure of this added part[15] until one recalls the ancient maxim that no more than two active characters shall normally appear on stage at one time, and that scenes are often divided by adherence to this rule.[16] It is then apparent that if we count the original miracle story as the first scene, the whole chapter is in its present form a kind of drama constructed with no small amount of skill:

1. Jesus, his disciples, and the blind man   vv. 1-7
2. The blind man and his neighbors   8-12
3. The blind man and the Pharisees   13-17

[14]Verses 3a-5 may also be material added to the original story. They link the miracle to the Johannine portrait of Jesus as the light of the world. Regarding the possible significance of the pronouns in v. 4, see below.

[15]Dodd, for example, divides chap. 9 into a narrative of healing (vv. 1-12) and a dialogue in the form of *a* trial scene (vv. 13-34), *Interpretation*, pp. 354 ff. (italics mine). Similar analyses are made by Barrett, *St. John*, pp. 292 ff., (miracle and narrative); Bernard, *St. John*, Vol. II, pp. 323 ff.; Hoskyns, *The Fourth Gospel*, pp. 350 ff.; and Bauer, *Johannes*, pp. 128 ff.

[16]See, for example, Bultmann, *History*, p. 188, wherein analyzing the style of the similitude, he remarks that "the law of stage duality is operative, i.e. only two persons speaking or acting come on at a time. . . . If more than two have to speak or act, they have to do it in separate successive scenes." Cf. also E. Haenchen, *Die Apostelgeschichte* (1965⁵), p. 96, n. 1, where the scene technique employed by Luke in Acts 25:13–26:32 is compared with style exemplified in Vergil. For our purposes it will be important to note that even in Luke 13:10-17, which is the closest parallel to John 9 in a number of important respects, there is only one scene. See excursus A on Luke 13:10-17.

He who reads the chapter aloud with an eye to the shifting scenes and the skillfully handled crescendos cannot fail to perceive the artistic sensitivity of the dramatist who created this piece out of the little healing story of verses 1-7. Moreover, reading it together with 5:1-18 (the healing of the lame man) and 18:28–19:16*a* (the trial before Pilate) will surely lead one to conclude that the skilled dramatist is the Evangelist himself. For there is virtual unanimity in crediting him with the construction of these other texts that are dominated by such similar scene-presentation. It is then the Evangelist who has created in John 9 a dramatic unity which captures and holds the reader's attention, and effectively prepares him for the important discourse of chapter 10.

We cannot be satisfied, however, merely to speak of the Evangelist's art. We must ask whether in his composition it is possible to detect specific reflections of some definite situation in the life of his church. To this end we may find it illuminating to formulate our questions as we transpose the narrative into a more developed dramatic form.[19]

2. Transposition into Dramatic Form

In the dramatic rendering of chapter 9 that follows, the reader who compares the drama with the text as it stands in the Gospel will soon perceive certain modifications. With one exception each of these modifications is relatively minor and, therefore, will either be explained in a footnote or simply allowed to "bear

[17]In vv. 18 and 22 the term οι ιουδαιοι stands instead of the expected φαρισαιοι. The change may be significant (see suggestion below), but it must not be taken as evidence of a literary seam. Note that the term φαρισαιοι returns in v. 40. Compare also 1:19, 24.

[18]Cf. Bent Noack, *Zur johanneischen Tradition* (1954), p. 115, who finds eight scenes by allowing a division after v. 5. After making the above analysis several years ago, I was pleased to find that the chapter was translated in seven scenes by J. M. Thompson, and that Thompson's lead was followed by Windisch. See the works cited above in note 5.

[19]In order to conserve space and facilitate communication this will be done partly by synopsis. The reader is referred to the full text for comparison.

witness to itself." The exception, the "doubling" of Jesus with an early Christian preacher, may strike some readers as a bold step indeed. Therefore, before we proceed, a word must be said in its defense.

In the Farewell Discourses which Jesus makes to his disciples following the last supper there is the surprising promise:

> Truly, truly, I say to you, he who believes in me will also do the works that I do . . . because I go to the Father. (14:12)

From this promise it is a short step indeed back to 9:4:

> It is necessary for *us* to work the works of him who sent *me* while it is day.[20]

The work of Jesus appears not to be terminated in the time of his earthly life. On the contrary, his going to the Father inaugurates a time in which his followers do his works. Indeed, 9:4a leads us to see this continuation of Jesus' works as an activity of the Risen Lord in the deeds of Christian witnesses.

We must take into account, however, the whole of John 9:4. While the grammatical incongruity introduced by the pronouns in the first half of the verse "us . . . me"—points to the continued activity of the Risen Lord in the work of Christian witnesses, the second half of the verse clearly speaks of a time when it will be impossible for anyone to work, and verse 5 continues this motif:

> We must work the works of him who sent me, while it is day; night comes, when no one can work. While I am in the world, I am the light of the world.

If the Johannine church lives in this night—that is to say, if in an absolute sense Jesus has departed from the world—then we must recognize a sharp contradiction between John 9:4a and 14:12 on the one hand, and John 9:4b-5 on the other.

I am confident that the problem thus posed is a real one. In John's view Jesus does return to the Father. More than once Jesus announced the termination of his sojourn:

---

[20]The MS witness is divided on both pronouns (see Bernard, *St. John*, Vol. II, p. 325 f.), but the convergence of (a) Bengel's maxim, *proclivi lectioni praestat ardua* with (b) the rule to prefer the reading which most easily accounts for the origin of the others tips the balance in favor of the reading presented by B and D. The profound implication purveyed by the Evangelist's use of the two pronouns ημας and με was sacrificed for easy clarity at an early date. Compare the highly significant change from singular to plural in 3:11.

Jesus then said, "I shall be with you a little longer, and then I go to him who sent me." (7:33; cf. 12:35; 13:33; 14:19; 16:16) It is not surprising, therefore, to find interpreters saying such things as:

The "night" was coming for him in this sense only, that when his public ministry on earth was ended, the "works" which it exhibited would no longer be possible.[21]

But while I am confident that the problem posed by Jesus' departure to the Father is a real one, I am equally confident that the Johannine church would emphatically deny that Jesus is now absent from the world in an absolute sense. John has not the slightest intention of limiting his message to the affirmation that during Jesus' earthly lifetime he *was* the Light of the World. Quite the contrary. Jesus makes his presence powerfully known—in what way we must carefully consider at a later point (chap. 7)—in his consistent declaration: "I am." For the time being, therefore, we must carefully consider the implications of 9:4*a*:

It is necessary for *us* to work the works of him who sent *me*.

Immediately surrounding this verse is the original healing story in which Jesus works the works of God (vv. 1-7). But this occurrence is not terminated in Jesus' earthly lifetime, as the expansion of the simple healing narrative in verses 8-41 makes clear. Or to put it another way, the seam which we have discovered between verses 7 and 8 has literary, historical, and theological importance. In the material which follows verse 7 the Evangelist has extended the *Einmalig*,[22] not because he

---

[21]J. H. Bernard, *St. John*, Vol. II, p. 326. Cf. R. H. Lightfoot, *St. John's Gospel*, ed. C. F. Evans (1956), p. 202.

[22]Here and subsequently I use this German term for the simple reason that (even with help) I have not been able to think of a suitable English equivalent. By it I mean something like "back there" as opposed to "now and here." It must be clear that I do not at all mean its use to be related to the neo-orthodox "once for all." I wish only to distinguish two levels in John's way of presenting certain parts of his Gospel. The reader will not go far wrong if he renders my use of *einmalig* by the expression "once upon a time." I should also say that I have in mind something rather different from Cullmann's thesis regarding Johannine expressions which have double meanings: "Der johanneische Gebrauch doppeldeutiger Ausdrücke als Schlüssel zum Verständnis des vierten Evangeliums," *ThZ*, 4 (1958), pp. 360-72. Contrast also Cullmann, *Salvation in History* (1967), pp. 270 ff. Concerning the Evangelist's own stance toward what I have termed the two levels of his presentations see pp. 88 f. and 137 f.

discovered additional information about what the Earthly Jesus did on this occasion, but rather because he wishes to show how the Risen Lord continues his earthly ministry in the work of his servant, the Christian preacher.

In what follows, therefore, we will have to keep constantly in mind that the text presents its witness on two levels: (1) It is a witness to an *einmalig* event during Jesus' earthly lifetime. Though we cannot a priori limit this witness entirely to verses 1-7, it will be safe to assume the original healing story as its major locus. (2) The text is also a witness to Jesus' powerful presence in actual events experienced by the Johannine church. We may initially assume this to be the case throughout the whole of the chapter, though the degree to which it may be demonstrated will vary. Where the two levels of witness overlie one another (primarily in the first seven verses) one does not hope to distinguish them with absolute clarity. The bulk of the miracle story's dramatic expansion, however, betrays this second kind of witness, and will therefore demand our most careful attention.

3. The Drama

Scene 1: A street in Jerusalem near the Temple (in the Jewish Quarter of John's city?): verses 1-7[23]

Confronted by a blind beggar near the Temple, Jesus takes the initiative to heal him. However, the work of him who is the Light of the World (8:12, etc.) is not terminated in that deed. Through a faithful witness *in the Johannine church,* the healing power of Jesus touches a poor Jew, afflicted many years with blindness.[24] His sight is restored!

Scene 2: Near the man's home (the Jewish Quarter?): verses 8-12.

The man's neighbors and acquaintances, fellow members of the synagogue, are divided in their appraisal of the situation.[25]

[23]The reader is asked to keep the text of John 9 close at hand and to refer to the appropriate section *before* reading the synopsis or dramatic form of each scene given here. The correspondence indicated by the parentheses should be taken at this point as nothing more than a suggestion. Cf. below pp. 73, n. 100 and 84 f.

[24]Whether on the contemporary level of the text we are to think of physical as well as spiritual blindness is not clear. Cf. 2 Cor. 3:12-18.

[25]The motif of divided opinion among synagogue members is quite important, as further developments will show.

A Blind Beggar Receives His Sight

Some are convinced that the beggar has actually received his sight. Others cannot believe that this now-seeing man is the blind man. He must be someone who looks very much like the blind man. (In this way the reality of the miracle is confirmed for the reader.) The neighbors ask the man *how* he has come to see. He replies that a man called Jesus opened his eyes.[26] When they ask where Jesus is, he cannot say.[27] At this, the neighbors decide to take the man to their leaders,[28] men of mature judgment who can examine the case and arrive at definite conclusions.[29]

[26]One must allow for the fact that the form of the drama—as an occurrence involving Jesus himself—does not suggest as a natural course of events that the blind man should refer, let us say, to the power of Jesus' name. Nevertheless, his reply is consonant with the remarkable way in which the Johannine community was conscious not merely of Jesus' power, but also of his very presence. A comparison with Acts 3:6, 16; 4:10, 18, 30, where Jesus' name is the means of his present power, may reveal important theological distinctions between the Johannine and Lucan churches, not to speak of the primitive Jerusalem community. Cf. James 5:15; Mark 9:38.

[27]The neighbors' question may be quite significant to John. Cf. 7:32-36; 13:33.

[28]Cf. below, p. 116. John is well acquainted with persons who recognize the authority of those trained in midrash. Furthermore it may be of historical importance that rabbinic literature preserves several stories which refer to Christians healing Jews in the name of Jesus, and that in each case (as one would expect) halakic authorities intervene. The most famous is given in *Tosefta Hullin* 2, 22 (and parallel accounts elsewhere):

> It happened with R. Elazar ben Damah, whom a serpent bit, that Jacob, a man of Kefar Soma, came to heal him in the name of Yeshua ben Pantera; but R. Ishmael did not let him. He said, "You are not permitted, Ben Damah." He answered, "I will bring you proof that he may heal me." But he had no opportunity to bring proof, for he died. (Quoted from M. Goldstein, *Jesus*, pp. 32 f.)

Here a Jew wanted to be healed, even by a Christian's pronouncing the name of Jesus. However, a man of superior authority intervened. A similar story is recounted in *j Shabbath* 14d:

> The grandson [of R. Jehoshua ben Levi] had something stuck in his throat. Then came a man and whispered to him in the name of Jeshu Pandera, and he recovered. When he [the doctor] came out, he [R. Jehoshua] said to him, "What didst thou whisper to him?" He said to him, "A certain word." He said, "It had been better for him that he had died rather than this." And it happened thus to him, as it were an error that proceedeth from the ruler (Ecc. x. 5). (Quoted from Herford, *Christianity*, p. 108.)

The persons referred to here are relatively late (third century), but the attitude of R. Jehoshua may be instructive for our purpose.

[29]Who are these leaders? On the *einmalig* level, it may be that John 9:13-34 somehow reflects the author's knowledge of a Pharisaic Bet Din, as distinguished from the Sanhedrin. However, another solution seems more likely, i.e., that the text can be understood, as I have suggested above, only by recognizing the author's determination simultaneously to witness on both the *einmalig* and the contemporary levels. That is to say, the Pharisees in chapter 9 probably reflect the authority of the Bet Din in Jamnia much more than they reflect an historical "Pharisaic Sanhedrin" of Jesus' day.

31

Scene 3: The Sanhedrin of Jerusalem? (A meeting of the Gerousia[30] in John's city?): verses 13-17.

The neighbors bring the beggar to the authorites and then fade into the background or leave.

A voice from offstage informs the audience that it was a Sabbath on which the man was healed.

The Jewish authorities now take up the investigation by asking the man how he received his sight.[31] At his abbreviated answer (the reader of the drama has already heard the full answer), there is a division (σχισμα) among the leaders, reminiscent of the divided opinion among the neighbors. Some are convinced that the man's healer cannot be from God because he breaks the Sabbath. Others pose a question in his defense: "How can a man who is a sinner perform signs of this sort?" In this way the question turns from how the healing happened to *who* is the healer, i.e., what is one to say of him?

The leaders address this last question to the beggar; his answer provides the climax of scene 3: "He is a prophet."[32]

Scene 4: The same courtroom: verses 18-23.

Having answered the leaders' question, the beggar fades into the background, and then vanishes.

The Jewish authorities[33] summon the man's parents in order to continue the investigation.[34]

---

[30]Here and subsequently I use the transliterated Greek term "Gerousia" in order to refer to the ruling body of Jewish elders in John's city.

[31]On the *einmalig* level the "how" question is more immediately relevant than is the question of the healer's identity. Making a medicine by crushing or grinding was considered work and therefore prohibited on the sabbath. That the story moves around two questions *(how* and *who)* may be another indication of the two levels of reference presented in the text.

[32]Note the progression: Jesus is a prophet (v. 17), he is from God (v. 33), he is Son of Man (vv. 35-37). I should not say this is a progression in the identification of Jesus, but rather a progression from identification to confrontation. See below, pp. 128 and 150 f.

[33]The investigators are now called by the general term "the Jews." From this Wellhausen and Spitta concluded that vv. 18-23 were added by the Evangelist to his source. It may be more relevant to ask why the general term appears this *late* in the drama. According to our analysis in terms of the two-level witness, one might have expected it as early as v. 13. It is not John's method, however, to separate the two levels neatly, and that has considerable theological significance.

[34]Why do the authorities never summon the *healer* in order to question him? On the *einmalig* level alone, this question is not easily answered. In the synoptic tradition Jewish authorities always consider *Jesus* answerable for his actions. Note carefully the implications of Mark 3:2, "And they watched him, to see whether he would heal him on the sabbath, so that they might accuse him

Is this your son who you say was born blind?[35] How is it that he now sees?

The parents answer that he is their son, but they do not know how he has come by his sight. Then, as sometimes happens with frightened witnesses who know something dangerous to themselves, they volunteer a *lack* of information. They say that they do not know *who* opened their son's eyes, adding nervously, "Our son is of age, ask him!"

But the authorities had not asked them *who* healed their son.[36] Therefore from offstage a voice informs the audience that the parents did indeed know who had healed their son. And it is frightening to possess this particular knowledge, as they stand before the Jewish court. For they know *two* things: that the healer is Jesus, whom the Christians confess as Messiah, and that the Jews have already agreed that if any of their number confesses this Jesus to be Messiah, he will be put out of the synagogue.[37] This is why they are frightened, the voice repeats, and the audience can readily understand.[38]

[Jesus]." See also Excursus A on Luke 13:10-17. The same motif is present in John 5:16 (5:18 reflects two levels) and 7:23. It is strikingly absent in chap. 9 and in 10:19 ff. One must ask why this is the case. The reverse side of the coin also calls for explanation. In synoptic healing stories, the one healed is never subjected to critical examination.

[35]The demonstrative pronoun οὗτος may indicate that the beggar is still present. However, he plays no active part in vv. 18-23 and must be summoned a second time in v. 24.

[36]The answer goes beyond the question in a manner by means of which John is able to move once again to the center of his concern: the messianic identity of Jesus as it is discussed in John's own milieu.

[37]Cf. the discussion of exclusion from the synagogue given below. A good bit turns, of course, on the authorship of John 9:22. I have already identified the gifted dramatist responsible for verses 8–41 as the Evangelist himself. Most interpreters credit him with v. 22 as part of the drama. An exception should be noted: Brown, *John,* p. 380, tentatively allots vv. 22-23 to the fifth of the five literary stages through which he believes the Gospel to have passed, i.e., to the final redaction by someone other than the Evangelist. In making this tentative suggestion, Brown seems to be moved primarily by the "somewhat intrusive" nature of the verses. I can agree that they are somewhat parenthetical—Brown puts them in parenthesis in his translation—but their close relationship to v. 34 in this drama itself and to 12:42 and 16:2 elsewhere in the Gospel lead me to speak of them as an aside that is integral to the dramatic presentation.

[38]Perhaps one may recall the reference to Samuel the Small in *Berakoth* 28b. See p. 54. Note that on the *einmalig* level the messianic question is scarcely to be understood. As the story has developed prior to this point, confession of Jesus as Messiah has not even been mentioned as a possibility. Cf. Bultmann, *Johannes,* p. 254, n. 10.

With this tense note, the scene shifts.

Scene 5: The same courtroom: verses 24-34.

Having made little progress with the parents, the authorities accept their nervous suggestion and recall the beggar for further questioning. When he has come before the court, they continue:

> Give the praise to God. We know that this man [Jesus] is a sinner.

The beggar approaches the matter from a different point of view.

> Whether he is a sinner I don't know; but yesterday I was blind, and today I see!

Then the authorities resume their original tack, asking the beggar what the healer did to him, how his eyes were opened. The beggar answers:

> I've already told you, and you did not hearken. Why is it you want to hear the story again? Do you also want to become his disciples?

At this audacity the authorities revile the beggar in a way which reinforces the sharp dividing line already stated (v. 22).

> You are a disciple of that man, but we are disciples of Moses.

One must choose whether to be a disciple of Moses or of Jesus.[39]

> We know that God spoke to Moses, but as for this man, we don't know where he comes from.[40]

When the inquisitors admit ignorance regarding Jesus' origin, the beggar begins seriously to question their omniscience:

[39]In light of John 5:46 f., we may be certain this way of referring to the choice does not represent the Evangelist's own thought. "If you believed Moses (which a disciple of Moses should certainly do), you would believe in me. For he wrote about me." But if the thought does not come from the Evangelist, it must either be a means for heightening the drama—cf. Bultmann's expression in another connection, "notwendig für die Darstellung" (*Johannes,* p. 59, referring to "the Jews")—or else it accurately reflects the opinion of Jews known to John. Our analysis, it hardly need be said, favors the latter explanation. Cf. below, chap. 6.

[40]Cf. the Egerton Papyrus 2, where this statement is part of *direct dialogue* between the rulers of the people and Jesus: "Turning to the rulers of the people He spoke this saying: 'Search the Scriptures: those [scriptures] in which you suppose that you have life are the ones which bear witness concerning me. Do not think I have come to accuse you to my Father: your accuser is Moses, on whom you have set your hope.' And when they said, 'We know well that God spoke to Moses, but we do not know whence you come,' Jesus said in reply, 'Now your unbelief is accused.'" Cf. C. H. Dodd, "A New Gospel," pp. 12-52 in *New Testament Studies* (1953).

Why this is itself a marvel! You are learned men. He opened my eyes, and yet you do not know where he comes from. We know that God does not listen to sinners, but if anyone is a worshiper of God and does his will, God listens to him. Never since the world began has it been heard that anyone opened the eyes of one born blind. If this man were not from God, he could do nothing.

Such lengthy instruction from one of the ignorant Am ha-Aretz the synagogue authorities cannot tolerate! Has he not made a speech tantamount to the awful confession? Throw him out, as the agreement demands![41]

Scene 6: A street (near the meeting place of the Gerousia?): verses 35-38.

The Christian preacher who was instrumental in the man's healing hears that the man has been expelled from the fellowship of the synagogue. It is not an uncommon event in the experience of this preacher. He knows that even among the synagogue authorities themselves are some who believe the Christians' Jesus to be Messiah (12:42). To be sure, many of these are afraid to confess their faith just as this man's parents were afraid earlier today. All of them know of the dreaded agreement. To the preacher they are people who love the praise of man more than the praise of God (12:43). But he is not insensitive to their peril. Indeed, upon occasion, he must remind members of his own congregation that they will have to suffer persecution from the Jews (15:18 ff.). Some of them have been excluded from the synagogue just as this beggar now is (16:2). Indeed, some have been killed by Jews who thought they were serving God in their horrible action.

Now that the Christian herald has heard of the beggar's expulsion from the synagogue, he takes the initiative (as he had done in the first place—9:6) to find the man. They stand face to face in the street. The preacher knows that the man is just at the point of readiness for a genuine Christian confession, and so puts to him the decision of faith. The beggar responds readily with words addressed to his true healer: "Lord, I believe."

---

[41] A member of the Am ha-Aretz has failed to recognize the halakic authority of the Gerousia in regard to a most sensitive matter. Regarding the motif of casting one out, contrast 9:34 with 6:37.

Scene 7: The same street: verses 39-41.
Through his preacher-disciple, Jesus Christ speaks:

> For Judgment I came into this world, that those who do not see may see, and that those who see may become blind.

Some of the authorities, having left the synagogue, are standing nearby. They hear this saying and sarcastically apply it to themselves.

> Are we also blind?

The voice of the Risen Lord continues:

> If you were blind, you would have no guilt: but now that you say, "We see," your guilt remains.

The drama has reached its initial climax, but a sermon follows immediately:

> Truly, truly, I say unto you, he who does not enter the sheepfold by the door but climbs in by another way, that man is a thief and a robber. . . . I am the door of the sheep. All who came before me are thieves and robbers; but the sheep did not heed them. I am the door; if anyone enters by me, he will be saved.

2

He Is Excluded
from the Synagogue
and Enters the Church

"And they cast him out. . . .
'Lord, I believe.' "

Presented as a formal drama, and allowed to mount its actors, so to speak, on a two-level stage so that each is actually a pair of actors playing two parts simultaneously, John 9 impresses upon us its immediacy in such a way as strongly to suggest that some of its elements reflect actual experiences of the Johannine community. It does not strike one as artificially contrived, nor does it appear to be composed merely in order to dramatize a theological point of view. At least in part, it seems to reflect experiences in the dramatic interaction between the synagogue and the Johannine church. To observe these reflections one needs only to be aware of the two-level stage.

However, our imaginative presentation of the drama has left us with a number of unanswered questions. Consider the dramatis personae. Who are the pairs of actors playing identical roles on the two stages? In our dramatic transposition, answers have already been partially suggested, but these must be critically assessed and further developed. Furthermore—and for a student of Christian origins most important—what can we say about the circumstances surrounding the beggar's exclusion from the synagogue? Who are the "Jews" who have agreed that confession of Jesus as Messiah will bring about such exclusion? What is the exact nature of this awesome agreement? Are echoes of it to be found also in other literature of the time? What circumstances have led to its enactment, and by what means is it enforced?

Answers to such questions are essential if we are to arrive at anything like a clear picture of the situation in which John wrote his Gospel. Thus we propose to see whether data elsewhere in the Gospel can offer us additional clues; after that, we will find it helpful to turn our attention to the problem of relating the Johannine picture to information which may be gleaned from other Christian literature and from rabbinic sources as well.

1. Exclusion from the Synagogue According to the Fourth Gospel

a. Chapter 9 itself provides us, in this regard, with several essential points of information. Notice again verse 22, which reads in part:

> For the Jews had already agreed that if anyone should confess him to be Messiah, he would become an excommunicate from the synagogue.

Here four elements command our attention: (1) the expression "the Jews," (2) the verb with its adverbial modifier "had already agreed," (3) the messianic confession of Jesus, and (4) the predicate nominative "an excommunicate from the synagogue."

The first two elements show us clearly that the subject under discussion is a formal agreement or *decision* reached by some *authoritative Jewish group* (cf. the analysis of 12:42 below) at some time *prior* to John's writing. Within this group, whoever its members may be, the need for a decision has been felt, and that decision has been made.[42] We are not dealing with an *ad hoc* move on the part of the authorities who happen at the moment to be questioning the beggar and his parents.

We are also told that those whom the decision concerns are Jews who confess Jesus as the expected Messiah. They have evidently assumed that such a confession is compatible with continued membership in the synagogue. Now, however, after

---

[42]The syntax of John 9:22 may call for some attention. The verb συντίθημι could be completed by an infinitive, but where the subject of the complementary verb is a second party, one will not be surprised to find the ινα substitute. Thus: The Jews had already agreed that (ινα) a man should become an excommunicate from the synagogue if he should confess Jesus to be Messiah. For the infinitive complement, see Acts 23:20. Cf. Blass, Debrunner, and Funk, *Grammar,* §392; N. Turner, *A Grammer of New Testament Greek* (Moulton, Vol. III, *Syntax,* 1963), p. 142.

the agreement, the dual commitment is no longer possible. For we are also informed by the key term αποσυναγωγος (*aposynagogos:* an excommunicate from the synagogue) that the decision has as its purpose the formal separation of the disciples of Jesus from the synagogue. If there is doubt about this point, a moment's reflection on John 9:28 should suffice.

You are a disciple of that one[43] but we are disciples of Moses.

This statement is scarcely conceivable in Jesus' lifetime, since it recognizes discipleship to Jesus not only as antithetical, but also as somehow comparable, to discipleship to Moses. It is, on the other hand, easily understood under circumstances in which the synagogue has begun to view the Christian movement as an essential and more or less clearly distinguishable rival.[44] The agreement is, then, a formal one, reached by an authoritative body within Judaism, intended to separate the two rivals, and at John's writing it has already been in effect for some indeterminate time.

b. While the adjective αποσυναγωγος has not yet been found in *any* document other than the Fourth Gospel, it does occur there twice in addition to the instance in chapter 9. One of these occurrences falls in Jesus' Farewell Discourses to his disciples. In the latter part of chapter 15 Jesus speaks clearly about the world's hatred of him and of his followers afterward. Then, without advance notice, the hating world seems to become hostile Judaism, for Jesus says the world's hatred fulfills the saying written in *their* law: "They hated me without a cause" (Ps. 35:19). Almost immediately, he continues by assuring his followers:

I have spoken these things to you in order that you may not be shocked. They will cause you to be excommunicated from the

---

[43]The pronoun εκεινος (that one) is used contemptuously, as Blass, Debrunner, and Funk point out, *Grammar,* §291, 1.

[44]The Christ-versus-Moses motif is struck repeatedly in the Gospel, and constitutes, as we shall see, not only the nuclear expression of the synagogue-church rivalry, but also one of the key problems with which John himself wrestled. See chap. 6 below. For the present it is more important to note that expressions which reflect this feeling on the part of the synagogue are not lacking in rabbinic literature. See Herford, *Christianity,* p. 442, and for late but illuminating evidence, K. G. Kuhn "Giljonim und sifre minim," in Walter Eltester, ed., *Judentum, Urchristentum, Kirche* (1960).

synagoguge. . . . I did not tell you these things at first, because then I was with you. (16:1 ff.)

One scarcely needs to argue, especially in light of the last sentence quoted, that these are words of the Risen Lord, spoken to the Johannine community to guard them in the midst of specific problems. And the problem accented here is the one presented by exclusion from the synagogue.

Here two specific notes are added to our picture: This text makes it unmistakably clear that some members of the Johannine church have come to it from the synagogue via the formal step of exclusion from that body. Secondly, we learn that the adjective αποσυναγωγος may be employed not only with the verb meaning *to be* or *become* (γενεσθαι) as in 9:22, but also with the verb *to make* (ποιειν). The former corresponds to some such expression as "become an excommunicate"; the latter to "make (someone) an excommunicate." Thus, in 16:2 the word clearly gives a _characteristic_ of persons now members of the Johannine church. They have been made αποσυναγωγος, and they may thereafter be described by this adjective; they are αποσυναγω-γοι (ones excluded from the synagogue).

c. The third reference which calls for our attention follows closely on the heels of the awesome quotations from Isaiah regarding those who have not believed the report and whose eyes have been blinded (12:37 ff.). Isaiah said these things, comments the Evangelist, because he saw Jesus' glory; Isaiah spoke of Jesus. It is nevertheless true, John continues, that

many of the rulers believed in him, but on account of the Pharisees they made it a practice not to confess him,[45] lest they be excluded from the synagogue (12:42).

In the drama of chapter 9, fear of exclusion from the synagogue was experienced by the beggar's parents, presumably ordinary members of a local synagogue in John's city. Now we learn that many of the "rulers" believe in Jesus, but consistently avoid a confession because they fear that the "Pharisees" will bring about their exclusion from the synagogue.[46] No reference is

[45]The imperfect verb ωμολογουν may have some such force.
[46]Regarding the perplexing problems presented by this verse, see below, pp. 84 f.

made to a prior agreement, as such, but the writer clearly presupposes it. The issue is the same, messianic confession of Jesus, and the key expression is identical, αποσυναγωγος serving as the predicate adjective of the verb γενεσθαι. This final reference helps us to fill out the picture. At some time prior to John's writing, an authoritative body within Judaism reached a formal decision regarding messianic faith in Jesus. Henceforth, whoever confesses such faith is to be separated from the synagogue. Many Jews, even rulers, do in fact believe, but they manage somehow to conceal their faith, lest they be excluded from the company of their brethren. Others, like the blind beggar, clearly reveal their commitment and are cast out. Indeed, John's church has a number of members who have personally experienced the operation of the awesome agreement. They are Jewish excommunicates (αποσυναγωγοι).

From John himself, therefore, we gain a fairly coherent picture. The picture may, however, be coherent without being historical. Furthermore, the picture itself defines a number of perplexing problems.

Concerning the dramatis personae: John says there are Christian believers even among the rulers. These authoritative persons evidently take no part in Christian services of worship, preferring to maintain their standing in the synagogue fellowship. How, then, does John know of such people at all, and precisely who are they? Furthermore, if we have correctly translated John 12:42, how can these rulers *consistently avoid* making the decisive confession? They obviously find it possible to attend the synagogue services without exposing their faith that Jesus is Messiah. How is such a course of action possible? Another problem is presented to us when John employs the term "Pharisees" to refer either to those who are responsible for the fearful agreement or to those who enforce it. We have already called these persons an authoritative body within Judaism, but beyond the term "Pharisees," John does not tell us who they are. Are there clues which will enable us to identify these actors in the drama?

Finally, has the key expression "to be put out of the synagogue" (αποσυναγωγος γενεσθαι) a recoverable historical reference apart from John's Gospel? What circumstances have called for such a drastic step, and how is it executed? In light of these perplexing questions, we may eagerly welcome data from other sources which put us in touch with the same general period.

2. Exclusion from the Synagogue According to Other Sources

We are justified to suppose initially that the three Johannine references we have just investigated do in fact reflect some historical event or events. These events may, therefore, have left their mark on other early Christian documents. Indeed, if the basic component is formal exclusion from the synagogue, we may also reckon with the possibility that the practice will have left echoes not only in Christian documents but also in Jewish traditions which belong to the same general period. In any event, we may interrogate such traditions in quest of further information.

a. Because we have been concerned to this point only with the text of John (Greek), and because the contexts in which we found the key term αποσυναγωγος seemed to support as the basic meaning "excluded from the synagogue," we have not found it necessary to examine the word itself in detail. Now, however, we will consider not only other Christian documents but also Jewish sources, most of which were originally written in Hebrew or Aramaic, and, as we shall shortly see, the contexts in which the Jewish references lie are often of no help at all. Therefore it is necessary to sketch a minimal definition of the term αποσυναγωγος.

Like many Greek words this one is a compound, made from a preposition, away from (απο), and a noun, synagogue (συναγωγη). It is probably quite analogous to the word αποδημος which means "away from one's people,"[47] and while the matter is certainly speculative, one would not be greatly surprised if some papyrus should be discovered which shows the term αποσυναγωγος used to describe a lone Jew residing for a time as the sole Jewish inhabitant of a city which therefore lacked a synagogue. Such a man would be *away from* the *synagogue*. The term itself, therefore, does not seem to carry any fearsome denotation, other

[47]Blass, Debrunner, and Funk, *Grammar*, §120, 2.

than the natural concern any Jew might feel at being away from the fellowship of his synagogue.

The way in which John uses it however clearly shows, as we have seen, an awesome connotation. Accordingly, lexicographers have not hesitated to give as equivalents: "expelled from the synagogue"[48] and "aus der Synagoge ausgeschlossen."[49]

b. Beyond this minimal definition one is clearly involved in interpretation. While neither the Greek adjective nor any direct Semitic equivalent has been adduced from Jewish writings,[50] its basic reference to expulsion or exclusion from the synagogue has caused most interpreters to link it with some form of the Jewish *ban* mentioned in rabbinic literature. Bauer's full definition, for example, reads: "expelled from the synagogue, excommunicated, put under the curse or ban (חרם)."

Furthermore, if it is, as Moulton and Milligan suggest, "just the sort of word that would have to be coined for use in the Jewish community,"[51] one would expect it to bear some relation to known Jewish methods of discipline. Thus when one seeks to identify the term historically, the practice of the ban is the most obvious candidate.

1. *The case for identifying "excluded from the synagogue" with the Jewish ban.*

Here it will suffice to give the results of a discussion which may be followed more carefully in Excursus B below. It is clear from rabbinic sources that there were two kinds of ban, the *niddui,* the less severe, and the *cherem.* Following the lead of those expert in the study of Jewish life and thought, many Johannine commentators have seen in John 9:22; 12:42, and 16:2 references to one or the other of these types of Jewish ban.[52] Bauer's entry

---

[48]Liddell-Scott, *A Greek English Lexicon* (rev. ed., by Jones and McKenzie, 1940), p. 221.

[49]Walter Bauer, *Griechisch-Deutsches Wörterbuch zu den Schriften des Neuen Testaments* (1952⁴), p. 183.

[50]See, however, Schlatter's suggestion from *Numbers Sifre,* cited below in Excursus B.

[51]J. H. Moulton and G. Milligan, *The Vocabulary of the Greek Testament Illustrated from the Papyri and Other Non-literary Sources* (1914–30), p. 70. Of course the absence of the term in Jewish sources (it could have been used even in its Greek form in the Talmud!) might suggest that it was coined not by Jews but rather by Christians, perhaps even by someone in the Johannine church.

[52]Many commentators refer the reader to Schürer's discussion in *Jewish People,* Division II, Vol. II, pp. 60 ff.

quoted above casts a vote for linking the passages with the *cherem;* the great rabbinic scholar, Adolf Schlatter, on the other hand argued forcefully for the *niddui.* Neither identification is likely for the following reasons:

a. A recent study has shown that when the rabbinic materials are carefully dated, there is no reference to *cherem* with the meaning "excommunicate" or "ban" prior to the third century C.E.[53] That does not exclude the possibility of linking the Johannine references to this ban; it does make such a link improbable.

b. Furthermore, the *niddui* appears to have been used only in order to protect the purity of legal rulings, and thus—so far as I can see—it was usually employed against *scholars* who refused to follow the majority ruling of a scholarly court. In any event, the words of Paul Billerbeck seem accurately to represent this aspect of the picture.

In none of the material which we have surveyed does one find the synagogue ban used in order to expel repugnant elements from the synagogue. Furthermore, everything we have learned about the ban's purpose and results speaks against such a use. On the contrary, the ban is designed as an *inner*-synagogue means of discipline, the purpose of which is to correct a member of the synagogue by bringing him to a state of obedience to Torah and to Torah's representatives. This shows that the ban is intended to hold a man firmly *to* the synagogue. It is never employed to expel one from the synagogue.[54]

If we may recall our minimal definition of the term αποσυν-αγωγος above, the case for identifying this term with the Jewish ban as we know it must be considered inadequate at best. For the preposition *away from* (απο) shows clearly that whatever may be taking place, it is not a matter of *inner*-synagogue discipline.[55]

---

[53]Hunzinger, *Bannpraxis,* pp. 65 ff.
[54]Billerbeck, *Kommentar,* Vol. IV, pp. 329 f. (italics added).
[55]A full excommunication was apparently practiced at Qumran. See *ThWNT,* Vol. 7, pp. 848 f. and the passages from IQS cited there. They scarcely provide a significant parallel to the Johannine expression, however, as the author, W. Schrage, recognizes.

44

2. *"Excluded from the synagogue" refers to the kind of disciplinary action taken against Christians according to Acts.*

In a fascinating article which appeared prior to the discovery of the Dead Sea Scrolls, Erwin Goodenough argued strongly that the Fourth Gospel shows a decidedly primitive character and should be understood as a product "from the very early church, though of course nothing indicates any precise date."[56] Obviously a number of the passages in which "the Jews" play a dominant role, such as those we are now considering, are not friendly to such a thesis, and Goodenough had to take this fact into account. In attacking what he termed the "hidden premise" that John "could not" have. been written early, he said:

> The hidden premise has not always, of course, been hidden. So G. H. C. McGregor, *The Gospel of John,* 1928, pp. xxix f., says that the disputes with the "Jews," and such objections as "He makes himself equal to God"; "Art thou greater than our Father Abraham?"; "Can this man give us his flesh to eat?" come from a "later age." Of these *Jesus' attitude toward the "Jews" in John is most often taken to indicate that the Gospel is late.* . . . The bone of contention, Colwell rightly says, is that the Jews rejected Jesus as the Messiah and as a divine being; but this issue must have been clear by the time of the Pauline persecutions in Jerusalem, and so we need no late date to explain a group who felt themselves on this ground tragically rejected from Jewry. . . . *These references to "Jews" might have been written during, or at any time after, the Pauline persecution.*[57]

This is not, to be sure, a direct statement about our term αποσυναγωγος; it is one of the disappointing features of Goodenough's article that this highly important word is nowhere considered. Nevertheless the suggestion is close at hand that the kind of disciplinary action taken by Paul against the church provides at least the background of our Johannine references.

---

[56]E. R. Goodenough, "John A Primitive Gospel," *JBL,* 64 (1945), pp. 145-82 (p. 145).
[57]*Ibid.,* p. 147, n. 3.

This is a suggestion which certainly merits serious consideration. If the Johannine term αποσυναγωγος is not to be linked
with the Jewish ban, a means of discipline employed *within* the
synagogue fellowship, perhaps it is somehow related to the kind
of action taken against Christians pictured in the Acts of the
Apostles. We need, therefore, to consider (a) the activity of Paul
when he was a persecutor of the church, and (b) disciplinary steps
taken against Paul and his companions after he became a
Christian missioner.

a. Aside from the various historical problems which attend the
accounts of Paul's activity as a persecutor of the church, there is
one factor which so effectively separates these accounts from the
Johannine references as to leave very little reason for relating the
two. All the way from the arrest of Peter and John in chapter 3 to
Paul's appearance (now as a Christian) before the Sanhedrin in
chapter 23, Acts paints a picture in which Jewish authorities view
the church as essentially subject to Jewish law. That is to say, the
church is viewed by the Jewish authorities as a *sect,* a bothersome
one to be sure, but still a sect which remained within the bosom of
Judaism. This is nowhere more apparent than in the case of
Paul's activity as a persecutor. According to Acts 9:1-2 and 22:5,
Paul received from the high priest in Jerusalem letters addressed
to synagogues in Damascus authorizing him to bring to
Jerusalem for disciplinary action any belonging to "The Way."
One thinks also of Paul's own words (Gal. 1:13; cf. Phil. 3:6),
according to which he not only persecuted the church, but also
tried to destroy it (επορθουν αυτην). The fact remains that the
tactics portrayed in Acts 9 do not even hint at excommunication.
Indeed just the opposite. Those of The Way are to be disciplined,
however severely, apparently in order that they might be brought
"into line," made to conform to the authority of the Jerusalem
Sanhedrin. Nothing would seem to be further from Paul's mind,
as Luke portrays him here, than the severing of those of The Way
from (απο-συναγωγος) the household of Judaism.

But if Paul's own activity prior to his conversion furnishes no
help, may we not look to the kind of discipline to which he was
subjected after he became a Christian?

b. It is often reported in Acts that Paul and his companions

46

experienced opposition and even persecution from the Jews.[58] On some of these occasions, the treatment amounts to the inciting of a riot and can scarcely be linked with the kind of formal agreement we have seen in the Johannine passages. Other instances show a more orderly disciplinary action, and two of these call for brief attention:

In Pisidian Antioch the Jews persuade the city authorities "to drive Paul and Barnabas out of their district." This is surely an expulsion "out of." But it is out of the district, not out of the synagogue, and the actual disciplinarians are the secular authorities of Antioch, not "Pharisees."

Jews from Antioch and Iconium follow Paul to Lystra and stone him there. This is certainly serious discipline. It is, however, a regularly appointed means of punishment. There is no hint of excommunication.

The second of these instances calls to one's mind Paul's own words in 2 Corinthians 11:24, in which he clearly states that on more than one occasion he submitted to synagogue discipline.

Five times I have received from the hands of the Jews the forty lashes less one. Three times I have been beaten with rods; once I was stoned . . . in danger from my own people.

"In other words," comments Vielhauer, "as a Christian he acknowledged the synagogue's jurisdiction over himself.[59] With this Acts agrees. In the course of events, presented by Acts, as we

[58]13:45-50 (Jews in Pisidian Antioch incite persecution of Paul and Barnabas and persuade the city authorities to send them on their way: εξεβαλον αυτους απο των οριων αυτων); 14:2-6 (attempted stoning in Iconium); 14:19 (Jews follow Paul from Antioch and Iconium and stone him in Lystra); 17:5 ff. (Jews in Thessalonica set the city in an uproar against Paul and Silas); 17:13 (the same persons follow Paul to Beroea and again incite crowds against him); 18:6-7 (Jews in the Corinthians synagogue oppose and revile [βλασφημουν] Paul; he shakes out his garments and leaves this synagogue permanently, moving his "classroom" next door to the house of Titius Justus; Crispus, the ruler of the synagogue, becomes a Christian together with others; 18:12-17 (the Corinthian Jews accuse Paul before proconsul Gallio, and when the proconsul refuses to take part in the matter of Jewish law, they vent their feelings by beating their own leader, Sosthenes, the ruler of the synagogue); 19:9 (experiencing opposition in the Ephesian synagogue Paul withdraws from the disbelieving Jews and relocates in the hall of Tyrannus); 21:27 ff. (riot and arrest in Jerusalem); 23:30 ff. (hearing before the Sanhedrin, but at the command of the Roman Tribune); 23:12 ff. (a plot to kill Paul); chaps. 24 ff. (further hearing before Roman authorities).

[59]Ph. Vielhauer, "On the 'Paulinism' of Acts" (pp. 33-50, L. E. Keck and J. L. Martyn, eds. *Studies in Luke-Acts* [1966]), p. 38.

have previously remarked, the Jewish authorities consider the Christian sect and its leaders to be subject to Jewish law.[60] Furthermore, when Paul is subjected to an examination by the Sanhedrin (23:6 ff.), he identifies himself not as a Christian excommunicate, but rather as a Pharisee!

3. *Behind Luke's portrait of the parting of ways in Acts 18 and 19 stands an event which was in reality, excommunication from the synagogue.*

In the course of recounting Paul's activity in Corinth and in Ephesus, the author of Acts tells of Paul's withdrawing from synagogues in both cities, and in telling the story the author employs three very interesting expressions:

Having encountered opposition and even reviling in the Corinthian synagogue, Paul moved his teaching activity next door to a private house. The expression may be somewhat literally rendered, "And [1] *moving away from there* [the synagogue], he went to the house of a man named Titius Justus . . . next door to the synagogue" (Acts 18:7).

After similar developments in the Ephesian synagogue, it is reported that "Paul [2] *withdrew from them* and [3] *separated the disciples*" (Acts 19:9). The first two expressions are probably synonymous and seem to speak of *ad hoc* moves on Paul's part. The first of them is explicitly part of the Lucan refrain, "You have rejected the message; therefore we turn to the Gentiles." For this reason especially, one may ask whether the responsibility for a portrait in which Paul acts wholly on his own volition may not rest with Luke rather than with history. Perhaps Paul was in fact, to put it politely, invited to leave the synagogue. And if we note that the burden of his teaching prior to the rupture is stated to be that the Messiah is Jesus (18:5), the suggestion lies close at hand that, leaving aside the Christian retouching, we have here a picture showing the αποσυναγωγος agreement in action. Paul teaches that Jesus is Messiah. The agreement calls for excommunication in such cases. He is expelled. Either he himself, or a later Christian editor, puts it in a different light: he withdrew of his own volition.

The third expression may be treated in a similar way. In

---

[60]Cf. L. Goppelt, *Christentum und Judentum* (1954), p. 87.

Ephesus, Paul not only withdrew but also separated the Christian disciples from the synagogue. The verb rendered "separated" is the same word used in Luke's form of one of the beatitudes.

> Blessed are you when men hate you and when they exclude you and revile you and cast out your names as evil on account of the Son of Man. (Luke 6:22)

In the beatitude the Christians are passive recipients of an action which excludes them. May it not be the case that in Acts 19:9 Luke has given the initiative to Paul, when in fact it was the synagogue authorities who drew the line of separation? In other words, is it not conceivable that "move away from" the synagogue; "withdraw from" the Jews (of the synagogue); and "separate the disciples," are Christian expressions for what was really the Jewish action described in the expression "put (someone) out of the synagogue"?

This is surely a weighty suggestion, but it runs aground on two major objections. First, had Luke received a tradition according to which Paul had been put out of the Corinthian and Ephesian synagogues, he would probably have reported events in just that way. One of his concerns is to show that the Gentile mission resulted from God's express will *and* from the persistent rejection by the Jews. Nothing would have dramatized the latter more effectively than accounts of synagogue excommunication. Thus, one follows a very unlikely course if he changes the texts to show that the initiative for separation actually lay with the Jewish authorities rather than with Paul.

Second, the separation does not at all appear to have been the *formal* separation of two rivals. When Paul comes to Ephesus, even after the events in Corinth, he begins his work anew in the synagogue (18:19; 19:8). Later, when he lands in Palestine, he finds that the Christian Jews there have heard of his laxity regarding the Law; they have not been told either that he has been excommunicated or that he has permanently separated his followers from the synagogue (21:20 ff.). Nor are these possibilities even hinted at in any of the proceedings which constitute Paul's arrest and various trials and hearings. It is not impossible that there is some kind of connection between the

references in Acts 18–19 and the Johannine expression.[61] It is by
no means clear, however, that the two refer to the same course of
events, and we must therefore continue our quest for historical
identification.

**4. The formal separation between church and synagogue has been
accomplished in John's milieu by means closely related to the
Jewish Benediction Against Heretics.[62]**

If we recall the four key points in John 9:22—(1) a formal
decision, (2) made by Jewish authorities, (3) to bring against
Christian Jews, (4) the drastic measure of excommunication
from the synagogue—it is clear that the historical identifications
suggested thus far prove to be disappointing because each fails to
correspond to one or more of these points. A priori one may
believe that at some time in the first or second century Jewish
authorities in one or more locales reached an agreement to apply
the ban to Christian Jews as an inner-synagogue means of
discipline.[63] Since the ban as we know it in this period is,
however, an inner-synagogue means of discipline, this hypothesis scarcely satisfies the third point: excommunication from the
synagogue. Or again, to the reader of Paul's epistles and of Acts,
it is conceivable that the Apostle's activity evoked a hostility
leading to his excommunication. He certainly founded churches
in the diaspora which were completely separated from the
neighboring synagogues. This does not appear to have happened, however, by excommunication, but rather by Paul's own
decision. And even in the course of these events, Paul
understood himself to be subject to synagogue discipline,
therefore scarcely as an excommunicate. Furthermore, one
hears no hint in Acts of a formal agreement lying back of the
synagogue's hostility to Paul. On the contrary, such events as are

[61]It may be, for example, that particularly in Acts 18:5-8 we are given a series of
events of the kind which *led* to the agreement spoken of in John 9:22.
[62]Cf. K. L. Carroll, "The Fourth Gospel and the Exclusion of Christians from
the Synagogue," *BJRL* 40 (1957), 19-32; E. Grässer, "Die Antijüdische Polemik
im Johannesevangelium," *NTS* 11 (1964–65), 74-90; R. Kysar, *Fourth
Evangelist*, pp. 150-56 and the literature cited there. Also G. Forkman, *The limits
of the religious community. Expulsion from the religious community within the
Qumran sect, within Rabbinic Judaism, and within primitive Christianity* (1972).
[63]This move may, in fact, be reflected in Luke 6:22, as Hunzinger suggests,
Bannpraxis, p. 74.

narrated in Acts appear to be *ad hoc* measures taken in one city after another.

As we begin our fourth test case, we will do well, therefore, to pay close attention once again to each of the four elements of John 9:22. We are looking for a turn of events which may properly be termed a formal agreement or decision. Those responsible for the decision are Jewish authorities; John refers to them as "the Jews," and may refer to them also as "the Pharisees" (12:42). They view followers of Jesus and orthodox adherents of the synagogue as rivals, and the intention of their decision is to bring about complete separation of the two. Henceforth, one who makes the messianic confession of Jesus is to be excommunicated.

a. We begin with the verbal thought "to agree, to reach a corporate decision" (συντίθημι). If we are to consider Jewish sources, we must ask how Hebrew- and Aramaic-speaking Jews would have expressed this thought. There are, one must admit, several possibilities known to us. Delitzsch rendered it with the verb יעץ, which in ancient Hebrew meant to consult together or exchange counsel (Niphal).[64] The use of this verb appears to be rather limited, however, in post-biblical times, and in any event its meaning has shifted somewhat by the Tannaitic period, so that it is not a very happy choice.[65]

A more likely candidate is the verb תקן (Aramaic תקן), which means "to introduce a custom," or "to ordain." The Hebrew and Aramaic forms of this verb are often attested in the early Christian period and are used in a way which corresponds fairly closely to the verbal thought of John 9:22. For example:

> At the close of every Benediction in the Temple they used to say, "For everlasting"; but after the heretics [Sadducees?] had taught corruptly and said that there is but one world, they *ordained* that they should say, "From everlasting to everlasting." (*Mishna Berakoth* 9, 5)

Here an authoritative body (not specified) reacts to the threat of an heretical teaching by issuing a rule, by publishing a new decision. And the structure of the sentence is similar to that of

---

[64]Brown, Driver, and Briggs, *Hebrew and English Lexicon of the Old Testament* (1952), pp. 419 f.; cf. Jastrow, *Dictionary*, p. 585.

[65]The same may be said for the Aramaic equivalent יעט. See Jastrow, *Dictionary*, p. 584.

the sentence in John 9:22: "They ordained that . . ."; "The Jews decided that . . ."[66] This use of the verb תקן is rather common and corresponds to the use of the noun תקנה. For example:

This is one of the nine *enactments* (תקנות) of Rabbi Johanan ben Zakkai. (*Rosh Hashanah* 31*b*)

Indeed the term is itself a key to one of the most important developments in Judaism after the fall of Jerusalem and the destruction of the Temple in C.E. 70. In this period, introduced by a tragedy of earth-shaking proportions, the major threat to Judaism was that of disintegration. It is often remarked that the Judaism of Jesus' day was an ellipse, the two foci of which were the Temple and the Law. After C.E. 70, the saying continues, the ellipse became a circle whose center was the Law. There is some value to this statement, but it has the distinct liability of obscuring the extreme trauma and deep uncertainty that attended this transition. Prior to this "shaking of the foundations," Judaism was of a most varied nature. There were groups ranging from the left end to the right end of the political spectrum. There were wild-eyed zealots plotting imminent revolt against the Romans. There were others set on collaboration. And what we would call various positions on the religious spectrum were thoroughly intertwined with these political opinions. For most of these groups the Temple cult, with all its imperfections, was a decisive cohesive force. Now that was gone, and there arose the danger that centrifugal forces would shatter the loosely knit phenomenon of Judaism, leaving the pieces widely scattered indeed.

b. In these uncertain years which followed the fall of the Holy City, the major stabilizing force appears to have been provided by the rabbinic academy which assembled at Jamnia under Johanan ben Zakkai and by the series of enactments or *Takkanoth* which were issued from this relatively stable center of learning and authority.[67] It is just possible, therefore, that our

---

[66]The Hebrew reads: והתקינו.

[67]The *Takkanoth* are listed most conveniently on pp. 155 ff. of J. Neusner, *A Life of Rabban Yohanan Ben Zakkai* (1962). We can be sure that the rabbinical picture of the Jamnia Academy is idealized to some degree, but I think that the idealization does not materially affect the data on which the following arguments are based. See notably Goldin, "The Period of the Talmud," pp. 146-52, and cf. the following two notes.

search for a turn of events properly termed a formal decision and for an authoritative body in Judaism responsible for this decision should in fact lead us to the little town of Jamnia in the period after the destruction of the Temple. Is there, among the *Takkanoth* published by the Jamnia authorities, one that may reasonably be linked with the measure taken against Christian Jews and spoken of in the three Johannine references?

c. A famous passage in the Babylonian Talmud requires quotation here. In the service of worship ideally followed in every Pharisaic synagogue, a centrally important element was the formal prayer spoken by a member of the congregation who was appointed for that task on a given day. The wording of this prayer—called the Eighteen Benedictions—was not wholly fixed until long after the New Testament period, but it was an understandable concern of the Jamnia authorities to standardize it to some degree. This concern provides at least part of the background of the following passage:

> Our Rabbis taught: Simeon the cotton dealer arranged the eighteen benedictions in order in the presence of Rabban Gamaliel in Jamnia. (*Berakoth* 28*b*)

Rabban Gamaliel was the head of the Jamnia Academy from about C.E. 80 to about C.E. 115. Under his leadership the authority of the group of scholars assembled in Jamnia grew considerably, so that it came to view itself as indeed the successor to the old Sanhedrin of Jerusalem. Here we see the academy concerned to arrive at a fixed order for the Jewish prayer. Presumably it was equally concerned to publish this order via an official enactment *(Takkanah)* ideally binding on the order of worship in all synagogues. That was, in any event, standard procedure for the Jamnia Academy, and while some resented such high claims for authority, the claims seem to have been recognized fairly widely.[68] So much for the order of the

---

[68]Jamnia was hardly the sole locus of rabbinical activity and authority. Moreover the period under scrutiny was one during which there were surely synagogues of quite different types in various locales. In general, however, the rabbinical data would seem reliably to indicate a remarkable growth of Jamnian authority precisely under Gamaliel II. See J. Neusner, *A Life of Rabban Yohanan Ben Zakkai*(1962), p. 125; H. Mantel, *Studies in the History of the Sanhedrin*(1961), pp. 34-35. See also the patristic data mentioned below in notes 71 and 81, notably Justin's statement that the Jewish authorities had dispatched messengers "to every land" to report the outbreak of the Christian heresy (*Dialogue* 17).

Benedictions. On a subsequent occasion,

> Rabban Gamaliel said to the Sages: Is there one among you
> who can word a benediction relating to the Minim [heretics]?
> Samuel the Small arose and composed it. (*Berakoth 28b*)

Some circumstance has now caused Rabban Gamaliel to
request a reformulation of one of the Benedictions, that against
the *Minim* or heretics (the *Birkath ha-Minim*). A certain Samuel
is said to have responded, though on a subsequent occasion he
himself experienced difficulty with his own formulation:

> The next year he [Samuel] forgot it and tried for two or three
> hours to recall it, and they did not remove him [from his post as
> Delegate of the Congregation]. Why did they not remove him,
> seeing that Rab Judah has said in the name of Rab: If a reader
> made a mistake in any of the other benedictions, they do not
> remove him, but if in the benediction of the Minim, he is
> removed, because we suspect him of being a Min?—Samuel
> the Lesser is different, because he composed it. But is there
> not a fear that he may have recanted? Abaye said: We have a
> tradition that a good man does not become bad. (*Berakoth
> 28b-29a*)

Needless to say, a host of fascinating questions arise when one
ponders this passage. We must restrict ourselves for the moment
to four which bear directly on our present task.

1. Is there evidence that the reformulated Benediction was, in
   fact, published by the Jamnia Academy as a *Takkanah*
   which it intended for use in synagogues far and wide?
2. Was its reformulation directly related to the nascent
   Christian church?
3. What goal did Gamaliel II have in mind when he called for
   the rewording?
4. And how, precisely, was it envisaged that the reformulated
   Benediction would accomplish this goal?[69]

[69]These four questions are formulated on the assumption that the pertinent
scenes portrayed in *Berakoth* 28 do in fact put us in touch with discrete events
which transpired—more or less pictured—during the period of Gamaliel's

He Is Excluded from the Synagogue and Enters the Church

If the data do not call for affirmative answers to the first two questions and for answers related to excommunication of Christian Jews for the last two, we will need either to continue our quest or to admit that no historical identification of John 9:22, etc., seems to be possible.

The first question may be easily enough answered. Such an important measure would naturally have constituted an official enactment by the Jamnia Academy. To make decisions regarding the synagogue liturgy was one of the major prerogatives claimed by Jamnia.[70] Furthermore the rewording of part of *The* Prayer (Amidah = Eighteen Benedictions) would

---

ascendency in Jamnia. Wayne A. Meeks has kindly explained to me that the major grounds for his hesitation to link our Johannine texts to *Berakoth* 28 ("Man From Heaven," p. 55, n. 40) lie in his suspicion that these scenes portray as punctiliar events in Gamaliel's time what was actually a linear development stretching over a lengthy period and culminating in the pertinent formulation of the *Birkath ha-Minim,* perhaps quite a bit later than Gamaliel (private letter of July 19, 1977). I am inclined to take Meeks' skepticism seriously. There can be no doubt that a number of rabbinical texts present something like the sort of punctiliar "historicization" he believes may be present in this instance. However, for three reasons I have decided to remain with the case for the *probability* of a relationship between John 9:22 etc. and *Berakoth* 28:

1. The formal nature of the language in John 9:22 would seem to point to a development that John perceives as a formal agreement on the part of an authoritative Jewish body. See pp. 38 f. above. Of course that body could be the local Bet Din in John's city, but there is also

2. the remarkable degree of correspondence between the *two* elements mentioned in John 16:2 (1. excommunication and 2. execution) and the *two* measures referred to by Justin in *Dialogue* 16, 95, and 110 (1. curse = cast out and 2. kill). This correspondence would seem to indicate the probability that a *Takkanah* useful toward excommunication by means of cursing was issued rather widely prior to Justin's time, and that would seem to be what *Berakoth* 28 is about.

3. There is, moreover, the matter of the case for linking the second element in John 16:2 (execution) to rabbinical tradition about the nature of the charges that led to Jesus' death: see chapter 3 below. If one be convinced by the arguments given there, it follows that in reflecting upon the execution of Jewish Christians in his community John has used a frame of reference (the beguiler) which is absent from the remainder of the New Testament but mirrored quite accurately in rabbinical tradition. That does not tell us, of course, that his references to excommunication are definitely to be linked to a discrete event in Gamaliel's time, but it supports such an interpretation.

In sum, then, we are dealing with questions which can be resolved only with some degree of probability. Taking into account all of the pertinent data seems to me to indicate as probable that the *Birkath ha-Minim* was issued under Gamaliel II and that it is in some way reflected in John 9:22 etc.

[70]See, e.g., Goldin, "The Period of the Talmud," p. 150.

have had no purpose were it not published for use far and wide.[71]
We are not surprised, therefore, to read in the Talmud:

> The benediction relating to the Minim was *instituted* in Jamnia.
> (*Berakoth* 28*b*)

The verb is תקן; the wording of the Benediction Against Heretics was a *Takkanah,* published by the Jamnia Academy. The date, while not a matter to be fixed with complete certainty, is scarcely a subject for rank speculation. The outer limits are given by the inception and the final termination of Gamaliel's official ascendency in Jamnia, events which we can set at about C.E. 80 (the probable date of Johanan's death[72]) and about C.E. 115 (the date usually given for Gamaliel's own death, there being no indication that he lived to see the shattering event of the revolt under Trajan, ca. C.E. 116). Added precision would be possible if one could be confident that Samuel the Small (i.e. probably the humble) was extremely old when Gamaliel assumed office and was therefore unlikely to have lived past C.E. 90. The pertinent data on Samuel are subject to this interpretation,[73] even if they do not demand it. Hence most scholars date the rewording of the Benediction Against Heretics at about C.E. 85.[74] After consulting several colleagues particularly expert in such matters, I should be prepared to allow for a date between C.E. 85 and C.E. 115, with an inclination toward the earlier part of that period.[75]

---

[71]Weighty support for the thesis that the rewording of The Prayer was a Jamnian Takkanah which was widely published with remarkable effects is given by patristic data. See Justin, *Dialogue* 16, 17, 85, and 110; Eusebius, *H.E.* iv, 18, 7. For our present quest Justin's references are quite impressive, as three of them (*Dialogue* 16, 95, 110) seem to correspond quite closely to John 16:2. See notes 69 above and 78 and 81 below.

[72]J. Neusner, *A Life of Rabban Yohanan Ben Zakkai* (1962), p. 1972; Neusner, *Development of A Legend,* pp. 221-24.

[73]Herford, *Christianity,* pp. 128-35, argues that Samuel is likely to have died "very near the year A.D. 80," and while Herford's line of argument is punctuated with several suppositions, it is not lightly to be laid aside.

[74]Typical is the presentation in W. D. Davies, *The Setting of the Sermon on the Mount* (1964), pp. 275 f. See further bibliographical references there, and the discussion in C. K. Barrett, *The Gospel of John and Judaism* (1975), pp. 47 f.: "Anything that occurred in the period of Gamaliel occurred in the period of the Fourth Gospel."

[75]We will do well to distinguish two questions from one another: The probable date of the Benediction Against Heretics, and the degree of probability that may

He Is Excluded from the Synagogue and Enters the Church

Second, in order to consider who the *heretics* are and what goal Gamaliel may have had in mind with respect to them, we will need to have before us at least a close approximation to the wording of the Benediction as Samuel uttered it. For this we are, fortunately, not dependent on the modern Jewish Prayer Book, which in some of its parts reflects the hideous censorship imposed upon the Jews in the Middle Ages by Christian authorities. A

---

be enjoyed by the hypothesis of a relationship between the Benediction and John 9:22, etc. As regards the first, I have already mentioned the caution of W. A. Meeks (note 69 above). I have found instructive also the comments kindly offered by Morton Smith (private letter of July 11, 1977). Unlike Meeks, Smith interprets *Berakoth* 28 to reflect liturgical changes which actually took place under Gamaliel II, but he thinks it unlikely that Gamaliel would have attempted such reforms prior to the firm establishment of his power, a development which Smith places in the early second century. As in the case of the argument advanced by Meeks, I am inclined to take Smith's caveats very seriously. Regarding the question of the broad dating of the Benediction, I am now prepared to entertain the whole of the period between 80 C.E. and 115 C.E. But in spite of Smith's argument, I am not inclined to prefer the latter part of that period. As far as I can see, the rabbinical portrait of Gamaliel II is not that of a man who consistently exercised political modesty, waiting to see which way the wind would blow. On the contrary, during his first period as patriarch he seems in fact to have been something of an autocrat, so high-handed and so uncompromising as to have precipitated a revolt among the members of his academy and his own removal from office. Only after he subsequently demonstrated true colleagueship did they reinstate him. Moreover he may have begun to exercise considerable authority even before Yohanan's death. Cf. Neusner, *A Life of Rabban Yohanan Ben Zakkai,* p. 167.

With respect to the question whether there is a probable relationship between the Benediction and John 9:22, etc., Smith reasons as follows: The Benediction is to be dated in the latter part of Gamaliel's partriarchate (early second century), and that is too late for the Fourth Gospel. There remains, however, the possibility of an indirect connection: Gamaliel is likely to have instituted the *Birkath ha-Minim* after similar moves had been taken against Christian Jews in numerous communities, and perhaps the Jewish community known to the Fourth Evangelist was one of these. Hence the *Birkath ha-Minim* is "usable as an indication of the sort of thing John had in mind, but no more, and certainly not as a fixed point for dating." With regard to the case for a connection of some sort between the *Birkath* and John 9:22, etc., Smith and I do not seem to be very far apart. I remain convinced of its probability primarily for the three reasons stated above in note 69. Cf. also E. Lerle, "Liturgische Reformen des Synagogengottesdienstes als Antwort auf die judenchristliche Mission des ersten Jahrhunderts," *Nov. Test.* 10 (1968), 31-42. It would require an excursus to respond in detail to the fascinating arguments by which J. A. T. Robinson seeks to rebut those advanced in the first edition of the present work: *Redating the New Testament* (1976). As is fairly widely known, Robinson propounds the thesis that the Fourth Gospel—and indeed all of the writings in the New Testament—were written prior to A.D. 70. In the present note I can say only that Robinson's arguments seem to me to be designed to make water run uphill.

very early form of the whole prayer was discovered in 1896, and its Twelfth Benediction may be rendered as follows:

1. For the apostates let there be no hope
2. And let the arrogant government
3. be speedily uprooted in our days.
4. Let the Nazarenes [Christians] and the Minim [heretics] be destroyed in a moment
5. And let them be blotted out of the Book of Life and not be inscribed together with the righteous.
6. Blessed art thou, O Lord, who humblest the proud![76]

The first three lines (with line number 6) probably antedate the work of Samuel the Small. The "apostates" spoken of there were probably Jews who abandoned their faith in favor of the marvels of Hellenistic culture, which swept the Orient in the wake of Alexander's armies.[77] So also the words "arrogant government," while appropriate as a Jewish expression for Rome, are frequently encountered in the books of Maccabees as a means of referring to the Seleucid power personified in Antiochus IV "Epiphanes." The basic sentiments of these first three lines are precisely those of the famous 17th chapter of the Pharisaic *Psalms of Solomon,* written in the first century B.C.E. Thus, the task of Samuel the Small, at Gamaliel's direction, seems to have been to make an old benediction (lines 1-3, 6) relevant to the contemporary situation by specifying the new sources of danger (lines 4-5): Christian Jews and other heretics.[78] Henceforth, in the very center of Jewish worship, The Prayer, there is included a petition that God may cause Christian Jews (among others) to be

[76]A host of authors concern themselves with this text. A number of them are cited by J. Jocz, *The Jewish People,* pp. 51 ff. The Hebrew text and a most helpful discussion are given by K. G. Kuhn in *Achtzehngebet,* pp. 18 ff. I have followed Kuhn's lineation and find his discussion on the whole convincing.

[77]Kuhn, *Achtzehngebet.* See, e.g., 1 Macc. 1:11-15.

[78]That Christians are *included* among those who are cursed in the Benediction is placed almost beyond question by the term "Notzrim" (Nazarenes) and by the fact that several Church Fathers refer to a Jewish practice of cursing the Christians "while they read the prayers." The patristic texts are given conveniently in H. L. Strack, *Jesus, die Häretiker und die Christen* (1910), pp. 66*; see also Jocz, *The Jewish People,* p. 336 n. 257, who, however, does not accept the word "Notzrim" as part of the original text, and compare with the article by Lerle cited above in note 75.

destroyed and excluded from the Book of Life. The formulation is an official and authoritative decision, and it is directly related to the Christian movement.

Third, toward what goal, however, is it directed, and, fourth, how is it intended to function? Excommunication from the synagogue is not specified in the Benediction, but the words "let them be blotted out of the Book of Life" can scarcely have been spoken as an inner-synagogue means of discipline. Whoever utters this prayer asks for Jewish heretics a destiny wholly unthinkable for any member of the people of Israel. The Benediction is intended, therefore, to weld the whole of Judaism into a monolithic structure by *culling out* those elements which do not conform to the Pharisaic image of orthodoxy.[79]

How they are to be separated is not said either in the Benediction or in the Talmudic passages in which it is mentioned. We are not left, however, wholly to our imagination. We need only to place ourselves for a moment in the ancient synagogue service.[80] There we find ourselves face to face with three persons whose roles were probably central to the working out of the Benediction Against Heretics: The president of the synagogue (*Rosh ha-Keneset* = αρχισυναγωγος), the overseer (*Chazzan* = υπηρετης), and the delegate of the congregation *(Sheliach Zibbur)*. The last of these is not an official of the synagogue, but rather any adult male selected by the president and then actually invited by the overseer to lead the congregation in the recitation of the Eighteen Benedictions. A number of rabbinic passages enable us to surmise that for detecting heretics the Twelfth Benediction was employed in the following manner:

   a. A member of the synagogue does something to arouse suspicion regarding his orthodoxy (cf. John 3:2; 7:52*a*).
   b. The president instructs the overseer to appoint this man to

[79]Cf. Kuhn, *Achtzehngebet,* p. 20. Gamaliel's determination to subject to himself the distinguished scholars of his court soon led him into a bitter struggle with liberal elements in his own academy and to the temporary loss of his office. See, e.g., Goldin, "The Period of the Talmud," pp. 150 f.

[80]Cf. I. Elbogen, *Der jüdische Gottesdienst* (1924²); P. Levertoff, "Synagogue Worship in the First Century," K. W. Lowther Clarke, ed., *Liturgy and Worship* (1932); C. W. Dugmore, *The Influence of the Synagogue on the Divine Office* (1944); S. Krauss, *Synagogale Altertüner* (1922), invaluable; P. Billerbeck, "Ein Synagogengottesdienst in Jesu Tagen," *ZNW,* 55 (1964), pp. 143-61.

be the delegate of the congregation, i.e., to lead in the praying of the Eighteen Benedictions.

c. Unless the man has a means of avoiding the appointment, he must go before the Ark (Torah Nitch) and recite aloud all of the Eighteen Benedictions, pausing after each to await the congregation's Amen. All listen carefully to his recitation of Benediction number 12.

d. If he falters on number 12, the Benediction Against Heretics, he is removed from his praying (cf. *Berakoth* 28b-29a cited above). He is then, presumably, "drummed out" of the synagogue fellowship.[81]

In the Fourth Gospel we find references corresponding directly only to (a): John 3:2; 7:52a, etc.; perhaps to the first part of (c): John 12:42, i.e., a synagogue ruler may have been able, at least for a period, to avoid appointment as delegate;[82] and to the second part of (d): John 9:34. Taken as a whole, however, and placed in light of the argument already advanced, the identification appears to be highly probable. Thus John 9:22 would seem to be a case of ellipsis. Fully expressed it would read approximately as follows:

The parents feared the Jewish authorities, for the latter had

[81]Douglas R. A. Hare has argued against relating John 9:22, etc., to the Benediction on the grounds that the Benediction does not speak of putting one out of the synagogue: *The Theme of Jewish Persecution of Christians in the Gospel According to Matthew* (1967), pp. 54 f. I am impressed by Hare's argument, but I do not find it convincing. I suppose, as my expression "drummed out" suggests, that just as a delegate of the congregation who stumbled on Benediction number 12 would be removed frm his post, so perhaps after careful questioning of the sort portrayed in John 9, he would be excluded from the synagogue. Note that Justin appears to use interchangeably the expressions "curse (καταραομαι) in your synagogues all those who believe in Christ" (*Dialogue* 16) and "cast out (εκβαλλω) every Christian from his own property" (*Dialogue* 110). When we recall that the synagogue fellowship was a kind of corporation, holding property in common, the suggestion is close at hand that Justin used these two expressions interchangeably because he knew that the test Benediction was employed in a manner which culminated in exclusion from the synagogue.

[82]There are several passages in rabbinic literature which seem to tell us that persons desired, from time to time, to avoid appointment as delegate of the congregation: *Berakoth* 5, 3, "If a man went before the Ark [as delegate] and fell into error, another must take his place: none may decline at such a time. Where does he begin? At the beginning of the Benediction in which the other fell into error." Cf. *Megillah* 4, 8 (note the context). See also S. Krauss, *Synagogale Alt.*, pp. 129, 136 f. and the passages cited there. Those who declined appointment as delegate did so, no doubt, for various reasons, as the passages show.

already enacted a means whereby followers of Jesus could be detected among synagogue worshipers. From Jamnia had come the official wording of the Shemoneh Esre including the reworded Benediction Against Heretics. Henceforth anyone arousing suspicion could be put to a public test (as in steps a–d above),, as follows:

a. John 9:22 ηδη συνετεθεινтο (they had already agreed), refers to the action taken under Gamaliel II to reword the Birkath ha-Manim so as to make it an effective means for detecting Christian heresy. Thus "the Jews" in 9:22 would seem to be John's way of referring to the Jamnia Academy. Consider the remarkable correspondence between the following two passages:

> John 9:22: The Jews had already agreed that . . . *j Berakoth* 8*a:* The Wise Men of Jamnia have before now appointed the Benediction Against Heretics.

I am not at all suggesting that these two references are interdependent. Each is, however, a natural way of speaking about what may actually have been the same turn of events.

b. John 12:42, οι φαρισαιοι (the Pharisees), refers either to the messengers (Sheluchim) who delivered the newly formulated Benediction to the Jewish community in John's city, or to members of the local Gerousia who enforce this formulation, much to the discomfort of believing "rulers."[83] The latter escape detection, perhaps by seeing to it that others are appointed to lead in prayer.

c. John 16:2*a* merely tells us, as has already been indicated, that certain members of the Johannine church have been detected as Christian heretics (steps a–d above) and have been excommunicated from the synagogue.

Thus the Fourth Gospel affords us a picture of a Jewish community at a point not far removed from the end of the first century. As we get a glimpse of it, this community has been shaken by the introduction of a newly formulated means for detecting those Jews who want to hold a dual allegiance to Moses and to Jesus as Messiah. Even against the will of some of the

---

[83]Cf. Justin, *Dialogue,* 17 and 108.

synagogue leaders, the Heretic Benediction is now employed in order formally and irretrievably to separate such Jews from the synagogue. In the two-level drama of John 9, the man born blind plays not only the part a Jew in Jerusalem healed by Jesus of Nazareth, but also the part of Jews known to John who have become members of the separated church because of their messianic faith and because of the awesome Benediction.

Part II

After the Wall Is Erected: The Drama Continues

3

The Jewish-Christian Beguiler
Must Be Identified

"He is leading the people astray."

1. Introduction

We are now able to reconstruct with probability a series of stages in the relationship John's church has known with the neighboring Jewish community.[84]

a. While there is not a great deal of specific information about the very earliest days, it is reasonable to assume that Christian missioners came to the city and preached in the synagogue, saying, "We have found the Messiah" (1:41, 45, 49). Before very long a document in which a number of Jesus' miracles were narrated as messianic signs may have been composed for use in

[84]Cf. now Martyn, "Glimpses into the History of the Johannine Community," pp. 149-75 in de Jonge (ed.), *L'Evangile de Jean*; also published in Martyn, *The Gospel of John in Christian History* (1979). See further G. Richter, "Präsentische und futurische Eschatologie im 4. Evangelium," pp. 117-52 in P. Fiedler and D. Zeller (eds.), *Gegenwart und kommendes Reich* (1975), summarized by A. J. Mattill, Jr., "Johannine Communities Behind the Fourth Gospel: Georg Richter's Analysis," *Theological Studies* 38 (1977), 295-315; R. E. Brown, "Johannine Ecclesiology—The Community's Origins," *Interpretation* 31 (1977), 379-93; " 'Other Sheep Not of This Fold': The Johannine Perspective on Christian Diversity in the Late First Century," *JBL* 97 (1978), pp. 5-22. The picture that has been unfolding in these articles is now consolidated and enriched in Brown, *The Community of the Beloved Disciple* (1979). See also R. A. Culpepper, *The Johannine School* (1975); D. M. Smith, Jr., "Johannine Christianity," *NTS* 21 (1974-75), 222-48; R. Schnackenburg, "Die johanneische Gemeinde und ihre Geisterfahrung," R. Schnackenburg, J. Ernst, and J. Wanke (eds.), *Die Kirche des Anfangs* (1977), pp. 277-306; F. Vouga, *Le cadre historique et l'intention théologique de Jean* (1977).

this early stage of evangelism.[85] We will return to this possibility at a later point. In any case, people believed and came therefore to form a messianic group within the synagogue. It is important to note that this group did not consider itself to be an entity socially distinct from the synagogue fellowship.[86] Presumably there were some separate meetings for celebrating the Eucharist and also for special teaching. Yet John 6 may show us that at one stage the Eucharist was made a subject of debate *both in the regular synagogue meetings* (vv. 25-59) *and in the separate gatherings of messianic believers* (vv. 60-71).[87] If so, that may be in part a reflection of this early stage in which the Jewish believers did not wholly abandon the regular synagogue worship.[88] While they must have known that their actions were beginning to be of some concern to the Jewish authorities, they obviously assumed that a dual allegiance to the regular synagogue fellowship and to their special group was possible. Thus, when they continued to mission among their fellows, they did not think of their work as that of drawing persons away from the religion of their fathers or from the synagogue itself. They were Jews, children of Abraham, and yet also disciples of Jesus the Messiah.

b. At some point the authorities came to view the messianic believers with added concern. Indeed they felt themselves compelled to conclude that belief in Jesus as Messiah was in reality apostasy. Perhaps official messengers came from Jamnia with the reworded Benediction Against Heretics and with instructions about its intended use. Perhaps, conversely, reports sent to Jamnia by the very authorities in John's city played a role

[85]The most significant attempt to recover this hypothetical document is that of R. T. Fortna, *The Gospel of Signs,* A Reconstruction of the Narrative Source Underlying the Fourth Gospel (1970). See also the comments of M. E. Boismard on what he terms "Document C," *L'Evangile de Jean* (1977), and Excursus E in the present volume.

[86]It is a remarkable fact that, even in the completed Gospel as we have it, the Gentile mission seems to play no part in the Fourth Gospel *as an issue.* Jewish opposition to John's church is never presented as the result of the church's inclusion of non-Jews. Nor is the Torah as the way of salvation the kind of issue it was in Paul's experience.

[87]See note 219 below. *The debate is christological* cf. Brown — Community of Beloved Disciple

[88]John 6:51 ff. may also indicate that some Jewish believers (12:42) did not want to take the Eucharist. The attitudes of Christian Jews and of Jewish Christians toward the sacraments is a subject about which we know very little. But see J. Betz, "Der Abendsmahlskelch im Judenchristentum," pp. 109-32 in *Abhandlungen über Theologie und Kirche* (Festschrift K. Adam, 1952) and G. Strecker, *Das Judenchristentum in den Pseudoklementinen* (1958), pp. 196-212.

in Gamaliel's decision to have the Heretic Benediction brought up to date as a means of detecting Christians and others. In any event, the local Jewish authorities came at some point to view the growing numbers of "believing" Jews as a stream of apostates which had to be stopped. A dam had to be built; steps had to be taken to make it unmistakably clear that synagogue and church were formally separate and that any Jew who made the messianic confession would have to pay the price of absolute severance from the synagogue. The Benediction Against Heretics was employed for detecting such Jews, and they were promptly excommunicated. What had been an inner-synagogue *group of Christian Jews* now became—against its will—a separated *community of Jewish Christians.*

c. The threat of excommunication must have narrowed the stream of converts. The blind man's parents, for example, if we may assume them to have felt the attraction of their son's embryonic faith, choose to remain safely in the bosom of the synagogue. Synagogue elders believe, but now that an open confession of their faith will bring their excommunication, they remain at least socially on the old side of the separating wall. Even the threat of excommunication, however, does not halt the stream altogether. Some are willing to pay the price of severance and do so. The question then arises whether the Jewish authorities will view this remaining trickle (Is it only a trickle? Notice John 12:11, 19) as insignificant, or whether they will devise still more stringent means for halting the traffic altogether. Perhaps they will need to take measures not only against those now within the synagogue who are tempted to embrace the messianic faith, but also against those already excommunicated who insist on evangelizing among the Jewish populace.

d. The initial task with which we are concerned at this juncture is that of following the drama into what we may call its "fourth act." The authorities could not, in fact, view the matter as closed. Even in the face of excommunication, synagogue members continued to make the forbidden confession. Therefore, a step beyond excommunication was called for, and in light of John 16:2 we have no alternative but to conclude that this step was the imposition of the death penalty on at least some of the Jews who espoused the messianic faith.

They will put you out of the synagogues; indeed the hour is coming when whoever kills you will think he is offering service to God.[89]

This conclusion itself, however, brings with it a number of thorny problems. How did the Jewish authorities bring about the death of Jewish "believers"? On what grounds was such a move possible? After this move, did all synagogue members attracted to faith in Jesus have to fear execution as well as excommunication, or was this second step taken only against Jewish Christians (already excommunicated) who continued the Christian mission among Jews?

It would be impossible to answer these questions if our only clue consisted of 16:2*b*. On the other hand, 16:2*a,* as we have already seen, refers to an experience which so impressed John that he allowed it to be clearly reflected in dramatic form elsewhere in the Gospel (chap. 9). Should the same be true of 16:2*b,* we might indeed hope to find answers to our questions. But where shall we locate in John's Gospel a drama in which someone comes to believe in Jesus and is subsequently arrested, tried, and executed for his faith?

A moment's reflection will suffice to show that such a formulation of the problem is far too inflexible. As the final question above implies, the further step of execution *may* have been taken not against converts like the blind beggar, but rather against Jewish Christian preachers. And if that be true, we may look for a drama in which on the *einmalig* level murderous steps are taken against Jesus himself.[90]

Such considerations might lead us to focus our attention on the passion story. However, if one will read the whole Gospel through at a single sitting, he will be reminded that threats on Jesus' life begin long before the passion story. The earliest occurrence of the term accented in 16:2*b* (αποκτεινειν: to kill) is in 5:18 ("This is why the Jews sought all the more to kill him

[89]Cf. Justin, *Dialogue,* 16, 95, 110, 133. As mentioned earlier, these references seem to reflect the same two steps mentioned in John 16:2, and except in the final reference Justin places the two steps in the same order: (1) curse, and (2) put to death. *Dialogue* 95, for example, reads in part: "If you curse Him and those who believe in Him, and, whenever it is in your power, put them to death . . ."

[90]Cf. *Sanhedrin* 107*b*: Jesus is excommunicated. Herford, *Christianity,* pp. 50 ff.

. . ."). And this verse clearly reveals a two-level frame of reference, as we shall see momentarily. Indeed, a rereading of chapters 5 and 7 impresses one with the possibility that in those chapters John has presented dramatic pieces which are no less powerful and no less transparent to elements of his own setting than is the integrated drama of chapter 9. Therefore, just as we turned from 16:2*a* to chapter 9, we may now proceed from 16:2*b* to elements in chapters 5 and 7.

2. Pertinent Dramatic Elements in John 5 and 7

The literary structure of John 5–7, even apart from the famous disjunctures presented by John 6, is far more varied and complex than is that evidenced by the tightly and simply composed scenes in John 9. Interpreters are not even agreed as to whether John 5 begins a new section of the Gospel.[91] But there are clear indications in the text itself that numerous elements in John 7 continue events and motifs of John 5,[92] and for our purposes it is the literary nature of these elements that demands attention.

a. John 5:1-18

This text consists of a miracle story which John has expanded by means fundamentally analogous to those employed in John 9. The Evangelist is himself responsible for verse 1. The traditional miracle story is clearly located in Jerusalem; Jesus has just been in Galilee (4:46); he must be brought to Jerusalem. Verses 2-9*b* present the healing miracle which is certainly old tradition, retaining accurate topographical references not elsewhere found in the New Testament,[93] and showing the three elements so often encountered in healing stories:

[91]Brown, *John*, pp. 201 ff., represents the widely held view that John 5 (introduced by 4:46-54) begins a section which reaches through John 10. For a contrary analysis see the article by Talbert cited in our next note.

[92]See C. H. Talbert, "Artistry and Theology: An Analysis of the Architecture of John 1:1-5, 47," *CBQ* 32 (1970), 341-66. While Talbert has not convinced me that John 1:19–5:47 is a single literary unit structured according to *chiasmus*—the resulting analysis of John 5 seems extraordinarily unlikely—he has given me pause as regards my suggestion (in the first edition) of a distinct literary cycle stretching from 5:1 to 7:52. Hence I now delete that suggestion. What is essential for our historical quest is the two-level nature of the drama in John 5:1-18 and of pertinent dramatic elements in John 7.

[93]See the fascinating study of J. Jeremias, *Die Wiederentdeckung von Bethesda* (1949). A summary in English is given by Barrett, *St. John*, pp. 209 ff. Jeremias' conclusions appear to be followed in the translation given by *NEB*.

1. The sickness is serious (v. 5).
2. Jesus heals the man (v. 8).
3. By carrying his pallet the man demonstrates the reality of his cure (v. 9*a-b*).

But now, in a way quite similar to that followed in the case of the blind man, John gives to the third of these elements a double role. In the original miracle story, the man's carrying of his pallet was indeed proof that he had been healed, and it still serves this purpose as the story is used by John. In addition, however, it provides a means whereby the story may be given a dramatic expansion.

By commenting that the day was a sabbath (v. 9*c*), John sets the stage for the drama. Now the man's carrying of his pallet constitutes not only proof of his cure but also a violation of the law excluding work on the sabbath, and the reader is prepared for a drama of conflict.

The drama has a sequence of scenes, not so clearly or exhaustively presented as those of John 9, but otherwise quite comparable:

Scene 1: In the House of the Flowing (Bethesda)[94] north of the Temple (vv. 2-9*b*).
Characters: Jesus and the crippled man.
Scene 2: In the neighborhood of Bethesda (vv. 9*c*-13).
Characters: The crippled man and the Jews.
Scene 3: In the Temple (v. 14).
Characters: Jesus and the crippled man.
Scene 4: Near the Temple (v. 15).
Characters: The crippled man and the Jews. (This scene is presented via editorial comment rather than direct discourse.)

One is tempted to find in verses 16-18 a fifth scene in which the actors are Jesus and the Jews.[95] However, if we are to think of a fifth scene at all, we should probably allot to it verses 16-47, and

---

[94]Brown, *John*, pp. 206 f., referring to evidence from the Qumran copper scroll.
[95]So Bent Noack, *Tradition*, pp. 114 f. Bultmann, *Johannes*, counts vv. 15-18 as one scene; Lindars, *John*, p. 52, calls vv. 9*b*–18 "a transitional dialogue."

we should then call it a sermon preached by Jesus to the Jews.

Does John present this drama on the two levels with which we are now familiar? We may note first that verse 16 is related to the drama on the *einmalig* level (just as Mark 3:6 is related to the story given in Mark 3:1-5).

> This is why the Jews persecuted Jesus, because he did this on the sabbath.

Jesus is a Jew. As such he is subject to Jewish law. Since he has broken the sabbath, he must be disciplined. The verb "persecute" (διωκω) goes, to be sure, beyond mere discipline. It looks toward the passion story, much as does the verb "destroy" (απολλυμι) in Mark 3:6. Nevertheless, verse 16 is wholly understandable in the *einmalig,* Palestinian frame of Jesus' life.

But now the Evangelist has Jesus defend his breach of sabbath law not by reminding his hearers that they water their cattle on the sabbath—a typical rabbinic manner of argument found precisely at this point in synoptic tradition (see particularly Luke 13:15)—but by uttering words which clearly imply a quasi-divine claim on his own part.

> My Father has never yet ceased his work, and I am working too. (v. 17)

And in the editorial comment that follows, the *two* levels of the drama are clearly and distinctly indicated.

> For this reason the Jews sought all the more to kill him, because he *not only* broke the sabbath, *but also* called God his Father, making himself equal with God. (v. 18)

There are reasons for seeking to kill Jesus during his earthly lifetime, and there are reasons for seeking to kill him now, in John's own day! To that we shall shortly return. For the moment, it is clear that the drama is presented on two levels, and we are therefore invited to sketch the essential elements of the contemporary level.

A member of John's church serves to make real in the life of a fellow Jew the healing power of Jesus. At that, the Jewish authorities step in and question the healed man.[96] Then, as in 9:35, the Jewish Christian finds the man and talks with him.

To this point, the drama corresponds very closely to that of John 9. There follow, however, two major developments which have no counterparts there.

1. When the Jewish Christian finds the healed man (v. 14), he does not lead him to a full Christian confession (contrast 9:35 f.), but rather gives him a solemn warning: "See, you are well! Sin no more, that nothing worse befall you." The warning represents good *Jewish* teaching. Why, then, does John place it here? The Christian senses the man's instability—i.e., that he might become an informer against his healer—and warns him not to fall into *that* sin lest something worse than sickness come to him.

It is therefore clear that the lame man of John 5 plays a role quite different from the one played by the blind man of John 9. *The blind man* represents for John the Jew whose experience of healing inclines him fundamentally toward faith in Jesus. In the course of his being examined by the Gerousia, he defends his healer, and the Gerousia responds by excommunicating him. *The lame man,* on the other hand, represents the Jew who, though presumably thankful to be healed, nevertheless remains wholly loyal to the synagogue. When members of the Gerousia ask him to identify his healer (5:12) and thus to participate, albeit passively, in whatever hostile steps they may take against the healer, he complies with their request.[97]

2. The Gerousia now begins a series of attempts to apprehend the Christian, and that is the second point at which the major line of chapter 5 diverges from that of chapter 9 (leaving aside, for the moment, developments in chapter 10). Once the lame man has demonstrated his loyalty to the synagogue by informing the Gerousia of his healer's identity, he drops out of sight. He is no

---

[96]It may be well to remind ourselves that this scene, just as the parallel scenes in John 9; has no counterpart in the synoptic tradition. In John's milieu Jews who have dealings with Christians are *always* interrogated. Cf. Herford, *Christianity,* pp. 103 ff.

[97]Neither the blind man nor his parents really cooperate with the Gerousia in chap. 9; when the parents feel their safety imperiled, they remain silent. The cripple, when he feels threatened (5:10), protects himself by informing against Jesus. Cf. John 11:57.

longer necessary to the drama, for now the Gerousia turns all its attention to the healer.[98]

These two points of divergence, taken in the context of extensive correspondence, tell us that *the impulse* which led John to construct the drama of 5:1-18 is similar to and yet also different from the impulse to which he responded in constructing that of 9:1-41. In John 5 the Evangelist intends from the outset to focus his reader's attention not on measures taken against the healed man, but rather on hostile steps taken against the Jewish Christian himself.

If we ask *why* the Gerousia wants to apprehend the Christian healer, we now hear two answers. One we have already deduced from 16:2. The threat of excommunication has not wholly stopped Christian conversions among synagogue members; the authorities conclude that in order to halt such conversions they must take steps against the separated Jewish Christians themselves. But should they be directly asked why they take these steps, they would answer, of course, in theological terms, and that is precisely what they do: "We persecute Jewish Christians because they worship Jesus as a second god!" (5:18*b*).

That answer may seem to clarify the picture, but in fact it only points to further problems. On what *legal grounds* can the Gerousia say that one who worships Jesus as a second god is to be killed?[99] Can the charge of worshiping Jesus really serve as the

---

[98]In this regard the drama of John 5 is more like synoptic healing stories than is that of John 9; i.e., the healed one drops from sight, and attention is turned to the healer. It is obviously important, however, to note the point at which the healed man fades from view. In the synoptic form, that happens immediately after he is healed; in John 5, it does not happen until he has informed against the healer. The similarity with synoptic healing stories is, therefore, superficial.

[99]This problem is particularly pressing in light of the fact that the Gerousia has already separated the Johannine community from the synagogue. I said above that the picture presented in Acts is that of a Jewish sect which remained under the authority of the Jewish hierarchy and that this picture does not readily correspond to the Johannine αποσυναγωγος γενεσθαι. Now I am on the verge of being compelled to conclude that in John's milieu Jewish leaders do in fact exercise some kind of authority even over those who have been excommunicated. I can only suggest that this authority exercised over excommunicates was of a very peculiar sort, carried out in light of what the Jewish leaders in John's city must have viewed as extremely provocative activity on the part of Jewish-Christian evangelists. This line of thought obviously presupposes that *within their own section of the city* the Jewish leaders had considerable *de facto* power. Perhaps their *de jure* authority in the city as a whole is reflected in John 18:31. "The Jews said to him [Pilate], 'It is not lawful for us to put any man to death.' "

basis for arrest, trial, and execution? Or do the authorities follow some route other than that of legal argument?

These are questions which the text does not as yet answer; we must, however, keep them firmly in mind as we proceed.

b. John 7

In Jerusalem Jesus has healed a cripple on the sabbath and has defended that deed by stating his uniquely close relationship to God. Both the deed and the statement (expanded into a sermon, 5:19-47) cause the Jews to seek to kill him. He therefore retires to Galilee (6:1; 7:1)[100] where, interestingly enough, he seems to be able to work and preach in safety (the feeding of the multitude; the walking on the sea; the discourse on the Bread of Life; reactions to the discourse which are varied but all nonthreatening). At 7:1 ff. Jesus is said to be reluctant to return to Jerusalem, and the reason given for his reluctance is quoted precisely from

[100]The famous problems posed by the order of events presented in John 5–6–7 as they presently stand are handled in several ways. See the commentaries. I accept the order as we have it. On the subject of "theological geography" in the Fourth Gospel see R. T. Fortna, "Theological Use of Locale in the Fourth Gospel," *ATR* Supp. Series 3 (1974), 95-112; and K. Matsunaga, "The Galileans in the Fourth Gospel," *Annual of the Japanese Biblical Institute* 2 (1976), 139-58. There are a few hints in the Gospel that would seem to indicate the presence in John's city of a distinct Jewish quarter. If so, one would think immediately of Rome, Antioch, and Alexandria. Concerning *Rome* see H. J. Leon, *The Jews of Ancient Rome* (1960), pp. 135 ff.; Philo spoke of "the great section (αποτομη) of Rome on the other side of the Tiber [which] is occupied and inhabited by Jews," *Legat.* 155. Concerning *Alexandria* see H. I. Bell, *Juden und Griechen im römischen Alexandreia, BÃO,* 9 (1926), pp. 10 ff.; Bell, "Alexandria," *JEA,* 13 (1927), pp. 171-84; by Philo's time the delta quarter did not suffice for the Jewish population, but the Jews in Alexandria were to a considerable extent judged by their own magistrates according to their own law: W. W. Tarn, *Hellenistic Civilization* (1952³, rev. G. T. Griffith), p. 221. Concerning *Antioch* see C. H. Kraeling, "The Jewish Community in Antioch," *JBL,* 51 (1932), pp. 130-60, especially pp. 141 ff.; G. Downey, *A History of Antioch in Syria* (1961), pp. 80, 447 ff., and Plate 11; B. M. Metzger, "Antioch-on-the-Orontes," pp. 313-30 in E. F. Campbell, Jr. and D. N. Freedman, eds., *The Biblical Archaeologist Reader,* 2 (1964), especially pp. 323 f. In the case of Alexandria, at least, the Jews *chose* to have their own quarter; the same was probably true in a number of other cities, though I should not at all exclude the possibility that the Fourth Gospel was written in Alexandria itself. See, for example, J. N. Sanders, *The Fourth Gospel in the Early Church* (1943), but contrast the same author's article on John's Gospel in *IDB.* To Sanders' arguments in favor of Alexandrian provenance as they are stated on pp. 165 f. of W. F. Howard, *The Fourth Gospel in Recent Criticism and Interpretation* (1955, rev. C. K. Barrett) should be added the existence of a Samaritan community in the city. See Schürer, *Jewish People,* index.

5:18—"the Jews" are seeking to kill him. Then, at the close of the initial paragraph (7:1-13) John tells his reader (1) that Jesus does in fact go up to Jerusalem, but in secret; (2) that "the Jews" are still seeking him; and (3) that among the crowd there are two opinions of Jesus, although for fear of "the Jews" (!) no one wishes to talk openly about him.

Clearly many problems of an obviously theological sort attend these verses, and it is certainly not my intention to suggest that the verses are wholly dictated by contemporary events known to the Johannine church. One point, however, obviously introduces the reader to subsequent developments in the drama of John 7, and it would seem to do so in a way that reflects the contemporary drama that is our present concern:

> While some said, "He is a good man," others said, "No, he is leading the people astray" (7:12; cf. 10:19).

We have already noted that 7:1 verbally repeats 5:18. For that reason we might expect to hear once again a discussion of the christological scandal of 5:18, i.e., that Jesus seems to be violating monotheism by making himself equal to God. Instead, the climax of the opening paragraph is created by the emergence of a division of opinion among the crowd which would not seem immediately to relate to Christology as such. We must therefore ask why John would introduce the notion of a "leading astray."

The question is especially pressing in light of the recurrence of this notion later in John 7. Doubly concerned by the tendency of many to believe in Jesus, the authorities dispatch their police to arrest him (vv. 31 f.). When the police fail to execute their orders, they are upbraided in sharp terms: "Are you led astray also?" (7:47). On the face of it the authorities are here speaking of their police as possibly being people who are led astray. But the authorities are also saying something quite decisive about Jesus, something which amounts to the second option posed in 7:12: Jesus is a person who leads people astray.[101]

[101]There is a passage in Hegesippus (quoted by Eusebius, *H.E.,* 2, 23, 4 ff.) in which the verb πλαναω appears, at first glance, to be used just as it is in John 7 (cf. also 2, 23, 10 with John 12:42!). A basic distinction is, however, more important. In Hegesippus' passage the verb is always passive, but with the middle meaning "to stray," "to err." In John, on the other hand, it is either active (7:12—Jesus leads persons astray) or passive with passive meaning (7:47—the police may have been led astray). This distinction is of fundamental importance, as I shall show in a moment. For in John the accent lies not on the peoples' "straying," but rather on a *technical charge* laid against Jesus: he leads people astray.

That statement might be made informally, or it might be an official accusation pointing to a process of law. In light of the pressing questions outlined above (pp. 72 f.), it will be important for us to discover, if possible, which is the case. And if it should turn out to look like an official accusation, we will need to learn at least two further things: where John got the picture of the legal process involved, and the precise law according to which the process is carried out.

Is it an informal expression of opinion or an official accusation? Supporting the former assumption is the fact that in 7:12 we are merely given two conflicting opinions held by factions in the Jerusalem crowd: "some said . . . ; others said. . . ." On the other hand, an atmosphere of legal proceedings is certainly provided when the Sanhedrin dispatches the police to arrest Jesus, and sits in council ready to subject him to a trial (note κρινειν in v. 51). Thus, the part of *the crowd* which expresses the negative reaction to Jesus may include *persons of authority*. Note 7:43, 44. A part of the crowd wants to arrest Jesus!

Moreover, note carefully the whole of the Pharisees' statement to the unsuccessful police:

Are you led astray also? (μη και υμεις πεπλανησθε)[102] Have any of the authorities or of the Pharisees believed in him? And do not tell us that the crowd (οχλος) has believed and that such a development argues in his behalf! For such people are ignorant of the law and are accursed [Am ha-Aretz]. (7:47 ff.)

It is now clear that the authorities are proceeding on the basis of Torah. The reason for the common people's being led astray is that they are ignorant of Torah. Had they an accurate knowledge of the law, they would not be taken in by this man. And that must mean that his actions are considered by the Sanhedrin to be against the law. He is apparently subject to arrest on the *legal charge* that "he is leading the people astray," i.e., he is leading them into the worship of a god alongside of God.

Where did John get the picture of this legal process? Is he following a piece of Christian tradition? Or did he, for reasons of his own, construct it out of his own head? Has it, like the term

---

[102]For an argument which supports the passive reading see Barrett, *St. John,* p. 274. The question may expect a negative answer; what is important, however, is that it has to be asked at all. It is a "cautious and tentative suggestion" (Barrett, p. 268).

αποσυναγωγος, a recoverable historical reference which we must consider to be an element in John's own setting? To answer these questions, we may proceed much as we did in the case of the term αποσυναγωγος, that is, by reducing them to a single question: Are there other sources which tell us of a legal process according to which one who leads people astray (to worship a god alongside of God) is subject to arrest, trial, and execution?

With respect to the New Testament that question is quickly enough answered. The Synoptic Gospels do not know of it as a legal procedure employed against Jesus or anyone else. They show only one dramatically developed attempt to arrest Jesus, the successful one, and the grounds on which the Sanhedrin proceeded in that instance were those of blasphemy and rebellion.[103] There is, to be sure, a highly interesting little story preserved in Matthew 27:62-66 in which the Sanhedrin or its representatives (the chief priests and the Pharisees) assemble before Pilate on the day following the crucifixion, in order to request that the tomb be made secure against a possible theft of the body.[104] In their request they refer to Jesus as "that deceiver" (ουτος ο πλανος), adding that should his disciples steal the body and claim a resurrection, the "final deception" (η εσχατη πλανη) would be worse than the first.

This is plainly a late piece of tradition in which elements of Jewish-Christian debate are reflected. And it may be important that it is the Sanhedrin which identifies Jesus as "that deceiver." Still, the story takes place after the crucifixion and refers primarily to the resurrection. The identification of Jesus as a deceiver does not at all appear to be a legal accusation, and, since it is made after his death, it certainly does not provide a basis on which the Sanhedrin contemplates taking action against him. It can scarcely provide direct illumination, therefore, for the legal process portrayed in John 7.

[103]In Mark 11:18; 12:12, and 14:1, the verb εζητουν is imperfect, and may refer not to attempted arrests (*RSV* is misleading in its rendering of 12:12), but to *plans* leading to the one, successful arrest (see *NEB*). Luke 20:19 (εζητησαν) does indeed refer to an attempted arrest. There is, however, no synoptic parallel to John's *dramatic portrayal* of an attempted arrest. On the grounds for Jesus' arrest, trial, and crucifixion, see M. Goguel, *The Life of Jesus* (1933), pp. 480 ff.; Paul Winter, *On the Trial of Jesus* (1961), pp. 49 f.; E. Lohse, *History of the Suffering and Death of Jesus Christ* (1967).

[104]On the combination "chief priests and Pharisees" (Matt. 27:62) see below, pp. 84 f.

Nor do we fare materially better when we widen our search to include other New Testament documents. Paul may have been called a deceiver (πλανος; 2 Cor. 6:8; cf. 1 Thess. 2:3), but there is little to indicate that a legal process was involved.

A bit more promising is a reference in Justin's *Dialogue* with Trypho:[105]

> The fountain of living water [cf. John 7:38; 4:10] which gushed forth from God upon a land devoid of the knowledge of God, the land of the Gentiles, that fountain is Christ, who appeared in the midst of your people [cf. John 1:11] and healed those who from birth were blind, deaf, and lame [cf. John 9 and 5]. He cured them by his word, causing them to walk, to hear and to see. By restoring the dead to life, he compelled the men of that day to recognize him [cf. John 12:11, 17-19].
>
> Yet though they saw these miraculous deeds, they attributed them to magical art [cf. John 8:48]. Indeed they dared to call him a magician (μαγος) and a deceiver of the people (λαοπλανος). But he performed these deeds to convince his future followers, that if anyone . . . should be faithful to his teaching, he would raise him up at his second coming . . . [cf. John 5:25]. (*Dialogue* 69)

Several observations are necessary regarding this passage. (1) In composing it, Justin may have depended on the Fourth Gospel. Not all of the motifs for which I have provided Johannine parallels are peculiar to John; Justin certainly drew on several sources for these two paragraphs. I am only suggesting that among these sources may have been the Fourth Gospel; and, if that should be the case, we must exercise extreme caution in suggesting that Justin offers independent historical data which illumine John 7.[106] (2) The statement that Jesus' contemporaries dared to call him a deceiver of the people (λαοπλανος) may depend on Matthew 27:63 (πλανος). We may recall Justin's obvious acquaintance with the Matthean passage in *Dialogue* 108. (3) However, there is one further note struck in *Dialogue* 69, which may very well prove to be a valuable clue. According to

[105]There are actually two references to Jesus as a "deceiver" in the *Dialogue,* but one of them (chap. 108) is obviously drawn from the Matthean story we have just considered and adds nothing important to it.

[106]On the question of Justin's possible acquaintance with John's Gospel see, e.g., R. Schackenburg, *Johannes,* Vol. I, p. 178. *Apology* 61:4 f. *may* be dependent on John 3:3 f. But see also A. J. Bellinzoni, *The Sayings of Jesus in the Writings of Justin Martyr* (1967), pp. 134 ff.

Justin, the Jews charge Jesus with being not only a deceiver of the people (λαοπλανος), but also a magician (μαγος). If Justin drew the former from Matthew 27 (and/or John 7:12), what is the source of the latter?

One may point to New Testament passages in which Jesus is said to cast out demons by the power of the prince of demons. But a far more likely source for Justin's word "magician" is precisely *Jewish tradition* of his own period. Indeed, it can scarcely be mere chance that in constructing a dialogue with a Jewish opponent, Justin here employs *the two terms* which reflect a considerable part of the basic attitude toward Jesus in rabbinic tradition. For the saying: "He *performed magic and misled Israel*" (*Sanhedrin* 107*b*) "contains *in nuce* the attitude of the tannaitic epoch (i, ii centuries) toward Jesus."[107]

Therefore, while Justin (like Matthew) does not show us a legal process connected with the word "beguiler" (πλανος), he does point us to Jewish tradition in which that term (its Hebrew equivalent, of course) is used to describe Jesus. What remains to be seen is (1) whether *the rabbis* used the term not only to *describe* Jesus, but also to designate a *legal charge* against him; and (2) whether that charge (leading astray) has specifically to do with *the worship of a god alongside of God.* Should both questions find an affirmative answer, we may be nearing an historical identification of the process shown in John 7.

One may have read many times the most famous "Jesus reference" in all of rabbinic literature. When one does so, however, with the present questions uppermost in mind, the pieces of the puzzle begin to fall into place. For in it we find not only that Jesus is said to have *led* Israel *astray;* we find also that this verb (together with two others) constitutes the *legal charge* laid against him by the Sanhedrin and therefore the grounds on which he is said to have been tried and executed. Moreover, the verb refers specifically to the act of enticing others into the worship of foreign gods![108] The passage is a commentary on the

[107]W. Bacher in the classic review of Herford's *Christianity, JQR,* 17 (1905), p. 180.

[108]I refer to the verb נדח, which in the passage in question shares its direct object with הסית. The two verbs are virtually indistinguishable in *Mishna Sanhedrin* 7, 10, which is the classic passage defining the offense; and the offense is explicitly that of the man who says, "I will worship [another god]. . . . Let us go and worship it." See also the second half of note 110 below.

78

The Jewish-Christian Beguiler Must Be Identified

Mishnaic teaching that prior to the stoning of one found guilty of a capital offense, a last attempt is made to locate defense witnesses.

> It was taught:[109] On the eve of the Passover they hanged Yeshu. And an announcer went out in front of him, for forty days (saying): "He is going to be stoned, because he *practiced magic* (כשף ≅ μαγω τεχνη πραττειν τι) and enticed (יסת) and *led* Israel *astray* (נדח ≅ πλαναω). Anyone who knows anything in his favor, let him come and plead in his behalf." But not having found anything in his favor, they hanged him on the eve of the Passover. (*Sanhedrin* 43a)[110]

This passage fairly bristles with problems with which we cannot now be concerned. Two comments are, however, necessary. (1) The first and last sentences are distinct from the remainder. As I have said above, the Mishnaic tradition being commented on has to do with *stoning,* and so also does the middle part of our passage. But the rabbis responsible for this tradition knew quite well that Jesus was not stoned, but rather hanged or crucified. Thus, they speak on the *einmalig* level only in the first and last sentences.[111] (2) Then why do they connect stoning with Jesus at all? The answer must be related to *the*

[109]A formula identifying what follows as old tradition, a *Baraitha.*

[110]The passage continues by giving the opinion of a rabbi of the late third century: "Ulla replied: Do you suppose he was one for whom a defense could be made? Was he not a deceiver (מסית ≅ πλανος) concerning whom scripture says, 'Neither shalt thou spare, neither shalt thou conceal him' (Deut. 13:9)." See also the Christian interpolation in *Testament of Levi* 16:3, and *Acts of Thomas* 48. The basic rabbinic teaching is *Mishnah Sanhedrin* 7, 10-11, where the three nouns are המסית (he who beguiles), המדיח (he who leads astray), and המכשף (he who practices magic). The first two are taken from Deut. 13, where they were clearly separate; in the *Mishnah* they have to some degree coalesced, and *taken together* they are the approximate equivalent of ο πλανος. [I say "to some degree," because there was rabbinic discussion about the distinctions between the two: see D. Hoffmann, *Mischnajot* (1968), IV, 178 n. 114.] If one takes "beguile" and "lead astray" as essentially a single matter, then there are two charges laid against Jesus in *Sanhedrin* 43a, as also in Justin, *Dialogue* 69: (1) μαγος = המכשף; and (2) λαοπλανος = המסית = המדיח.

[111]Note, incidentally, that the date given for the crucifixion agrees not with the synoptic but rather with the Johannine chronology, i.e., Nisan 14. See Barrett, *St. John,* pp. 39 ff., where, however, there is no reference to *Sanhedrin* 43a.

charges which are made in the body of the passage. It must either be the case that the rabbis who formulated this tradition made a *conceptual* connection between Jesus and a leading astray, etc., *or* that knowing of *Christians who were tried* on this charge (i.e., *Mesith; Maddiach*), they simply projected the procedure back to Jesus himself. If the second possibility should prove to be preferable, we should view *Sanhedrin 43a* as a composite reference to (a) the trial and stoning of Christians charged with "leading astray," and (b) the trial and crucifixion of Jesus. There is at least one good reason for preferring the second interpretation.

In rabbinic literature there are a number of passages which refer to a certain Ben Stada. Opinion is divided regarding the identification of this person. It cannot be doubted, however, that *some* of the rabbis incorrectly considered Ben Stada to be Jesus, and it is just this confusion of two persons which is important for our problem. I cite only one reference:

> The deceiver. . . . They place two witnesses in hiding in an inner part of the house and light a candle above him that they may see him and hear his voice. Thus they did to Ben Stada in Lydda: and they placed two scholars of the Sages as witnesses, and they brought him to the court and stoned him. (*j Sanhedrin 25c, d*)

This is a story about a specific event. A rabbi named Ben Stada lived in Lydda. He was suspected of being a *Mesith* (πλανος), was spied upon, brought to court, convicted on the charge of "enticing" or "leading astray," and stoned.

A passage in the Babylonian Talmud gives the same tradition, but to the sentence, "Thus they did to Ben Stada in Lydda," the remark is added:

> And they hanged him on the eve of the Passover. (*Sanhedrin 67a*)

Here is the same combining of stoning and hanging found in *Sanhedrin 43a,* but now it *plainly* involves two different persons. Ben Stada was convicted of "leading astray" and was accorded the punishment properly called for by that offense: stoning. A later hand has appended a sentence connecting that event with Jesus' crucifixion. Why was this connection made?

A number of answers are possible, and dogmatism is clearly out of place here.[112] It may be, however, that Ben Stada was, in fact, a rabbi who became a Jewish Christian. If he continued to train disciples, by imparting to them Christian teaching, the charge that he was a *Mesith* would indeed be correct. But hadn't Jesus himself taught the same doctrine? Yes. It would be easy, therefore, to "double" Ben Stada with Jesus.[113]

That is precisely what I am suggesting about the legal charge of "leading astray" in John 7. In portraying action taken against Jesus on the basis of this charge, John is not dependent on "Jesus-tradition," but rather primarily on his own experience. In his city the second and awesome step taken by the Jewish authorities (16:2*b*) was designed not to frighten synagogue members with the threat of excommunication, but rather to stop *Jewish*-Christians once for all from missioning among their own people. Do not such missioners persuade others to worship Jesus as a god alongside of God (5:18)? In spite of their having been excommunicated, they are, therefore, *in the technical and legal sense,* persons who lead the people astray. The law itself warns about them (Deut. 13:6 ff.) and provides the punishment due them. They are to be legally arrested, tried, and if found guilty, executed.[114]

---

[112]See the excellent discussion in Goldstein, *Jesus,* pp. 57-62, and add the reference to Schlatter in the next note.

[113]This line of thought first occurred to me as I read A. Schlatter's remarkable book, *Geschichte Israels* (1906). I quote Schlatter: "In Lydda kam ein Rabbiner in den Verdacht, er neige sich zum Christentum. Man liess ihn heimlich durch zwei Zeugen beobachten und als durch diese sein christlicher Glaube festgestellt werden konnte, wurde er gesteinigt" (p. 297; cf. p. 449 in the 3rd edition, 1925). It is also possible, of course, that Ben Stada was confused with Jesus not because he himself was a Christian, but because the only (or chief) cases of *Mesithim* known to certain rabbis were those involving Christians. Such an interpretation of *Sanhedrin* 67*a* would lend equal support to the suggestions I have offered above. Note also the latter part of *Sanhedrin* 43*a*: Jesus' disciples (of a latter period?) are condemned to death, though no charges are specified.

[114]The possibility of a second line of argument supporting this interpretation was suggested to me by Ed P. Sanders. I have developed it below in Excursus C. There is also corroborating evidence in the Pseudo-Clementine literature. See Martyn, "A Dark and Difficult Chapter in the History of Johannine Christianity," chapter 2 in *The Gospel of John in Christian History* (1979).

4

He Must Be Arrested and Tried by the Court

"The chief priests and Pharisees sent officers to arrest him."

It is now clear that in parts of John 5 and 7 we have before us pieces of a two-level drama much like the one found in John 9. Not only does the Gerousia in John's city subject members of the synagogue to sharp examination and even excommunication (the blind man). It also identifies Jewish-Christian evangelists as *Mesithim* (beguilers); and on the basis of that identification, it is able to institute legal proceedings against them.

The final verses of chapter 7 show us that Gerousia assembled, and fully prepared to hold trial. It develops, of course, that the Jewish Christian is not present. The scene is, nevertheless, constructed quite as compellingly as is any other scene in the Gospel. By taking us right into a meeting of the Gerousia, it provides the climax of the drama focused on the "beguiler."

I do not mean to suggest, of course, that the scene is a *report* of a meeting known to John. What we term a *report* of current events would probably be as inconceivable to John as would a report of events in Jesus' day. Nevertheless, we must consider the possibility that it *reflects* events and proceedings known to John, thus affording us further clues of considerable importance.[115]

Definite steps prepare the way for this final scene, and we must remind ourselves of them. John 7:30 is a general statement quite in the tradition of Mark 12:12.

[115]To distinguish tradition from redaction in John 7:45-52 may be virtually impossible. In any case, relying partly on the roles played by the various characters, I have suggested in Excursus D that the scene may not be entirely John's own creation.

He Must Be Arrested and Tried by the Court

And they tried to arrest him, but feared the multitude . . .

Then they tried to arrest him; but no one laid hands on him,[116] because his hour had not yet come. (John 7:30)

Reading these verses in their respective contexts will show, however, that John has altered the traditional formula in three ways: (1) In the Synoptics, the authorities fail to arrest Jesus because they fear the crowd. Jesus is very popular. One thinks twice before arresting a popular man. John, however, attributes the cause of their failure to the fact that in God's purpose the hour has not yet arrived for Jesus to die. (2) In the Synoptics, the failure is not immediately followed by the dispatching of officers for another attempt. John's interest in the contemporary level of his drama causes him to alter the tradition by introducing a second attempt immediately. (3) In the Synoptics, Jesus is shown to be popular among the Jerusalem crowd. So also in John. But, as we have just seen, for the Synoptic Evangelists Jesus' popularity provides the reason for the Sanhedrin's failure to arrest him. For John, on the other hand, Jesus' popularity (7:31 f.) is precisely the cause of their attempt to arrest him.

The first of these alterations is motivated by John's theological interests. The second and third clearly reflect the contemporary level of his drama. It is precisely the relative success of the Jewish-Christian evangelist which causes the local Jewish authorities to conclude that he must be arrested as a *Mesith*. They therefore dispatch police with orders to bring the Christian to the Gerousia for trial. But the police are awestruck by his words—the words of his master—and return to the Gerousia empty-handed, where they are severely upbraided for their failure. The judges reveal their own insecurity by entertaining the possibility that the officers have themselves fallen under the influence of the *Mesith,* as indeed the officers' statement might indicate: "No man ever spoke as this man speaks!"[117] And the

---

[116]Note the expression επιβαλλειν επι τινα την χειρα. It is used in the Synoptics to refer to Jesus' arrest (in Luke 20:19 to an attempted arrest) and to the arrest of Christians (Luke 21:12). The latter reference, Luke 21:12, points to its use in Acts (4:3; 5:18; 12:1; 21:27) to refer to arrests of Jewish Christians.

[117]See note 102 above. It is obvious that John intends his readers to sense in the question (7:47) a degree of insecurity on the part of the Pharisees.

judges' position is further compromised by the semi-defection of one of their own number, Nicodemus.

At this point caution is necessary. Have we not overstepped the bounds of probability? The drama may indeed reflect two levels *in general.* But do we not press the case too far if we take *these* developments as reflections of *actual* events in John's milieu? We have just seen how John allows his own *theological* interests to shape the story. Are we to think of the local Gerousia as actually dispatching police to arrest a member of John's congregation?

Answers to these questions hinge partly on an analysis of the way in which John portrays the characters in the drama. We must consider carefully the roles which they play and the names by which John refers to them.

1. The Chief Priests and the Pharisees (οι αρχιερεις και οι φαρισαιοι)

In John 5, the authorities are consistently called "the Jews." So also in John 7, *until* we come to the part of the drama in which the attempted arrest is portrayed. Then there steps onto the stage a group of powerful men, having command of a police force, able to hold court, and referred to as "the chief priests and the Pharisees." Who are these men? They obviously constitute the Sanhedrin. But just for that reason we must recognize that the expression "chief priests and Pharisees" is a *very strange* combination.[118] One would not be surprised to hear the Sanhedrin referred to as "the chief priests and the elders,"[119] for the men so designated were members of the Sanhedrin *in their capacity as* chief priests and elders. And since the former represented the dominant force in the Sanhedrin, it was even possible to employ the term "the chief priests" as *an historically accurate* shorthand expression for that body.[120]

[118]The combination is found only in Matthew (twice; it refers to the Sanhedrin) and in John (five times; always the Sanhedrin) among New Testament documents. See also Josephus, *Vita,* 21. For an interpretation of the expression in Matthew and in John, see R. Hummel, *Die Auseinandersetzung,* p. 16, where I learned of the passage in Josephus. I am pleased to find that, on the whole, Hummel's understanding coincides with my own.

[119]This expression is often so used in the New Testament, as in other literature of the time.

[120]See Acts 9:14 and Bauer, *Lexicon,* p. 112.

Allegiance to the Pharisaic party, on the other hand, cut across the proper distinctions in the Sanhedrin. Certain chief priests were not only members of the Sanhedrin but also of the Pharisaic party. John's reference to the Sanhedrin as "the chief priests and the Pharisees" is, therefore, an historically confusing reference. It is as strange as would be a reference to a modern seminary faculty as "the ministers and Presbyterians." Indeed some might be neither, and that too reminds us that "the elders" are completely left aside in John's formula. Why, then, does John employ such a strange expression?

The answer probably lies in his determination simultaneously to bear witness on two levels. The chief priests were the authorities of the Temple in which Jesus preached; they were the leading men of the Jerusalem Sanhedrin, prior to the fall of the Holy City. By mentioning them John cares for the *einmalig* level of his drama, for they are contemporaries of the earthly Jesus.

In John's own time, on the other hand, the reins of Jewish authority are held to a large extent by the Pharisaic Bet Din in Jamnia, and, on the local scene, by a Gerousia, the majority of whose members are (or appear to John to be) Pharisees. In mentioning them John has before his eyes the Gerousia which attempts to try Jewish-Christian missioners for "leading astray" members of the synagogue. Thus the two-level witness is accomplished by an unhistorical juxtaposing of two terms; the resultant expression refers *simultaneously* to the Jerusalem Sanhedrin of Jesus' day and to the Gerousia of John's city.

2. Police Officers (υπηρεται)

When the Sanhedrin (Gerousia) desires to subject Jesus (the Christian missioner) to a trial, it dispatches police officers to arrest him. The Greek term is υπηρετης, the Hebrew equivalent of which would presumably be חזן *(Chazzan)*.[121]

Here John does not need to juxtapose two terms. He has been able to effect the double level with a single term. For *Chazzanim* may equally well refer to the Levitical Temple police, who were at the beck and call of the Sanhedrin (via its high priestly

[121]Delitzsch's selection of משרתים is less likely. Evidently חזן was translated by νεωκορος as well as by υπηρετης. See V. A. Tcherikover, *Corpus Papyrorum Judaicarum* (1957-), Vol. I, p. 239, item 129, line 7. The reference in Tcherikover was called to my attention by Ed P. Sanders.

members), *and* to the beadles of a local court, among whose functions may have been that of summoning litigants for trial before a local Gerousia.[122] The double level of the drama is apparent in verses 32 and 45: In verse 32 the *Chazzanim* are police officers subject to the authority of the chief priests *(einmalig)* and of the Pharisees (contemporary). But when, in verse 45, the *Chazzanim* are sharply questioned by their superiors and even suspected of being led astray by the very *Mesith* whom they should have brought for trial, the superiors are simply called "the Pharisees."

It is apparent, therefore, that in constructing the final scene (7:45 ff.), John concentrates his view on the contemporary level of the drama. To his eyes the power in the local Gerousia lies with members who belong to the Pharisaic *chabura,* and these men do actually dispatch *Chazzanim* to arrest Jewish Christians charged with being *Mesithim.*

3. The Rulers (οι αρχοντες = αλλοι of 9:16)

Like the preceding word, this term is a perfect selection for a two-level frame of reference. In the plural it can properly refer to members of the Jerusalem Sanhedrin or to authorities in any city who are members of the local Gerousia.[123] Presumably John could have referred to the Sanhedrin/Gerousia by using this term; indeed, in 7:26 he apparently does just that. Elsewhere, however, he prefers the term "The Pharisees," and there may, indeed, be a reason for his preference. The Gerousia with which he is acquainted is dominantly loyal to the authority of Pharisaic Jamnia. That is why he can refer to the Gerousia with the single

---

[122]A local Gerousia had its own *Chazzan* and its own scribe. The latter recorded the pleas, arguments, verdicts, etc.; the former had several duties which apparently included being dispatched to summon the litigants. See *Shabbath,* 56*a,* and Krauss, *Synagogale Alt.,* pp. 121 ff. In a middle-sized city the Gerousia could have two scribes and two *Chazzanim.* See also Sylvan D. Schwartzman, "How Well Did the Synoptic Evangelists Know the Synagogue?" *HUCA,* 24 (1952-53), pp. 115-32. The article on "Synagogue" in the Hastings dictionary was written by W. Bacher and is the source of the *Shabbath* reference given above.

[123]See Bauer, *Lexicon* on αρχων 2.a. Schürer, *Jewish People,* Vol. II, part 2, pp. 244 ff., and Krauss, *Synogogale Alt.,* pp. 146 ff., do not wholly agree on the precise meaning of αρχοντες. See also H. J. Leon, *The Jews of Ancient Rome* (1960), pp. 174 ff. The Fourth Evangelist's use of the expression could be taken to refer either to the Gerousia of a single synagogue or to the Gerousia of a city. For our purpose the choice does not greatly matter.

term "the Pharisees." The Jamnia Loyalists who enforce the Benediction Against Heretics *are,* for all practical purposes, the Gerousia.

But John knows that even among members of the Gerousia there are secret believers (12:42), and he may have employed a term by which he can speak about them.[124] Perhaps he consistently refers to these persons as "rulers." Since the term is used only four times, this hypothesis may be easily tested:[125]

Nicodemus is a "ruler of the Jews" (3:1), and it is obvious that for John he is typical of those in the Gerousia who secretly believe. He visits Jesus by night as an earnest inquirer; he defends Jesus in a meeting of the Gerousia, even though that causes his colleagues to look on him with suspicion; he joins the synoptic Joseph of Arimathea in the task of tenderly burying Jesus. This final reference to Nicodemus is particularly telling. Joseph of Arimathea is "a disciple of Jesus" whose errand of pious mercy must be executed "secretly, for fear of the Jews." When John joins Nicodemus to this figure, he tells his reader quite plainly that Nicodemus is to be understood as a secret believer.[126]

In 7:26 the term is used to refer to the Sanhedrin/Gerousia. But here John thinks not of the majority (the Jamnia Loyalists), but of the silent minority which does, in fact, know Jesus to be Messiah.

In both of the remaining references (7:48 and 12:42), "the rulers" are carefully distinguished from "the Pharisees." Though

---

[124]I do not mean to imply that John intended his readers to analyze the dramatis personae as we are now doing that. See the last paragraph of the present chapter.

[125]In 12:31, 14:30, and 16:11, when John speaks of "the ruler [singular] of this world," he means Satan. The use of the plural is clearly distinct from the use of the singular.

[126]Perhaps the old and much discussed question whether John's Nicodemus bears some relation to the Nakdimon ben Gorion and/or the Buni of rabbinic tradition should be reopened. Most of the discussion has been carried out on the assumption that for Nakdimon to be significantly related to Nicodemus, he would have to be a contemporary of Jesus. But if we read the references in John 3, 7, and 19 as parts of the two-level witness, a significant relation requires not that Nakdimon be a contemporary of Jesus, but rather that he be a near-contemporary of the Fourth Evangelist. His being alive, therefore, in A.D. 70 is no problem at all. That he is not said to have been a teacher is, however, problematic. And the relevant *Beraitha* in *Sanhedrin* 43a is far from clear. See the discussion in J. Jeremias, *Jerusalem zur Zeit Jesu* (1963³), p. 110 n. (and index); Billerbeck, *Kommentar,* Vol. II, pp. 412-19; Klausner, *Jesus,* pp. 29 f.; Herford, *Christianity,* pp. 90 ff.; Goldstein, *Jesus,* pp. 31 f., 111 ff.

both are members of the Gerousia, the rulers fear the Pharisees! If both terms can refer, on occasion, to the whole of the Gerousia, why should they be carefully distinguished? Because "the rulers" (in 12:42, "many of the rulers") is John's shorthand for the secretly believing members of the Gerousia, while "the Pharisees" is his term for the Loyalists who dominate that body.[127] Thus when he allows the Pharisees to say to their *Chazzanim*, "Have any of *the rulers* or of *the Pharisees* believed in him?" (7:48), his choice of words reflects the fact that there is indeed a division (σχισμα) in the Gerousia itself. Some of the members (= the rulers) do believe, as Nicodemus shortly proves, yet without making the awesome confession which would lead to their excommunication at the hands of the majority.

It is now clear that the scale of probability is once again tipped in favor of the two-level drama. I do not suggest that the dramatis personae can be explained in no other way. I do think the path we have taken is the most probable one, especially in light of our

---

[127]I am tempted to suggest that in a paraphrase of 12:42 the term οι φαρισαιοι be used twice.

Many of the members of the Gerousia (αρχοντες) believed. But they did not confess their faith. For the Pharisaic apostles (οι φαρισαιοι = השלוחים) came from Jamnia with the reworded Benediction Against Heretics, and the majority of the Gerousia (οι φαρισαιοι) employed it as was intended: to excommunicate Christians from the synagogue.

Cf. *Dialogue* 137:

Agree with us, therefore, and do not insult (λοιδορεω) the Son of God; ignoring your Pharisaic teachers (φαρισαιοι διδασκαλοι), do not scorn the King of Israel as your synagogue presidents instruct you to do after prayers. Are these Pharisaic teachers the *Sheluchim* from Jamnia? They seem to be distinguished from the (local?) authorities (αρχισυναγωγοι) who enforce the Benediction Against Heretics. In any case, one must consider this possibility in light of the famous passage in Epiphanius (39, 11) in which the author speaks of a certain Joseph, a Jewish apostle, who was dispatched with epistles to Cilicia. In virtue of his apostleship he is said to have deposed and removed from office "many wicked chiefs of synagogues." Harnack (*The Mission and Expansion of Christianity*, Vol. I, 1908, p. 330) summarizes the picture of Jewish apostles gained from this and other references as follows: "(1) they were consecrated persons of a very high rank; (2) they were sent out into the Diaspora to collect tribute for headquarters; (3) they brought encyclical letters with them, kept the Diaspora in touch with the centre, and, informed of the intentions of the latter (or of the patriarch), received orders about any dangerous movement, and had to organize resistance to it; (4) they exercised certain powers of surveillance and discipline in the Diaspora; and (5) on returning to their own country, they formed a sort of council which aided the patriarch in supervising the interest of the law." Note also Juster's comment about the Patriarchal apostles: "Ces fonctionnaires avaient une compétence très étendue. Ils étaient chargés de contrôler les magistrats des communautés . . ." (*Les Juifs*, Vol. I, p. 389).

previous discoveries of the two-level type of drama in John. Sometimes John presented the two levels by using a single word for a corresponding pair of actors (υπηρεται; αρχοντες). Sometimes he did so by an unhistorical juxtaposing of two terms (οι αρχιερεις και οι φαρισαιοι). In either case, John was neither playing a kind of code-game, nor trying to instruct members of his church about points of correspondence between the Jewish hierarchy of Jesus' day and that of their own day. One may be confident that he did not intend his readers to analyze the dramatis personae in the way in which we have done it. Indeed, I doubt that he was himself *analytically conscious* of what I have termed the two-level drama, for his major concern in this regard was to bear witness to the essential *integrity* of the *einmalig* drama of Jesus' earthly life and the contemporary drama in which the Risen Lord acts through his servants.

5

Yet the Conversation Continues

"Why are you listening to him?"

To say, in light of the discoveries we have now made, that the relationship between John's Jewish-Christian community and the neighboring synagogue was filled with tension is clearly a case of understatement. While we certainly do not have sufficient data to be able to speak about the whole of that relationship, one thing is quite apparent. The dominant force in the Jewish community has felt it necessary to insulate the synagogue as effectively as possible from John's church. The Gerousia in John's city knows that to (1) the threat of excommunication and (2) the legal process carried out against Jewish-Christian missioners must be added (3) the plea that synagogue members not even converse with Christians.[128] Those who utter the pained cry of John 10:20, "Why are you listening to him?" probably correspond closely to the rabbis whom Trypho refers to as:

> our teachers who warned us not be on familiar terms with you Christians, nor to converse with you on these subjects. (*Dialogue* 38, 1)

In John's milieu, the dominant opinion on the Jewish side may have been that it was a sin even to listen to words spoken by a Christian.[129]

---

[128]I have commented above on the question of chronological sequence (see pp. 64 ff.). Perhaps the plea that synagogue members not converse with Christians was made at an early stage. In that case, the plea will probably have been reemphasized again and again, as other measures failed to bring desired results.

[129]Cf. the famous story of R. Eliezer's arrest for heresy, usually dated about C.E. 109 (Herford, *Christianity*, pp. 137 ff.; Goldstein, *Jesus*, pp. 39 ff.; Barrett, *The Gospel of John and Judaism*, p. 69, n. 39). Schlatter's comment, on the basis on that story, was: "Man hielt es auf der judischen Seite für Sünde, ein christliches Wort auch nur anzuhören" (*Geschichte Israels* [1906], p. 297). See also *Qoheleth Rabba* 1, 8.

It is equally clear, however, that by the time of John's writing, the insulating process has not yet met with complete success. Jewish Christians still make their way among synagogue members, and it is all too obvious from the pleading question of John 10:20 that some of those members *are* listening to what the missioners say. Thus, even in a situation in which conversation can lead to excommunication for the synagogue member and to arrest and trial for the Jewish-Christian missioner, the two still engage in discourse.

Precisely what do they talk about? We may begin to answer that question by recalling the contemporary dimensions of the two-level drama. Obviously they discuss the issue of Jesus' identity: Is he the Messiah? We have seen that the question takes various forms. In the excommunication drama of John 9, the titles "Prophet," "Messiah," and "Son of Man" appear. We will not speak, just now, of the relationships among these titles; it is enough to recall that excommunication is clearly said to follow upon confession of Jesus as *Messiah.* In the beguiler drama of John 5 and 7 the christological accent falls initially on the title "Son of God," but as the drama unfolds, we encounter the other titles as well. In the climax of that drama theological honors are shared by the titles "Messiah" and "Prophet" (7:40-52). It is clear that the issue of Jesus' messiahship stands at the center of the synagogue-church discussion. Indeed the more we read John's Gospel with this issue in mind, the more obvious it is that the title "Messiah" occupies an important place in the whole of John's thought. Consider two relevant passages:

> When Andrew, Peter's brother, accepts the Baptist's witness to Jesus and follows him, he also speaks to his brother about Jesus.

> "We have found the Messiah (which means Christ)." (1:41)

> In the course of her conversation with Jesus, the woman of Samaria says: "I know that Messiah is coming (he who is called Christ)." (4:25)

In view of the frequency with which the title "Messiah" is employed in modern conversations and writings about the New Testament, one is surprised to learn that John is the only New Testament author who employs the title itself.

To be sure, he translates it, and that fact may seem to militate against the thesis that he writes in a way which reflects actual intercourse between Jews and Jewish Christians. Would not Jews, of all people, be well acquainted with this title in its original form (reproduced in Greek transliteration)? One may answer, of course, that he offers the translation for the sake of his non-Jewish readers. But it is also possible that even among his Jewish readers are persons for whom the Hebrew tongue is a foreign language. It is well known that one of the most creative Jewish thinkers of the first century, Philo of Alexandria, was not able to read or write the sacred tongue; it is not difficult to imagine that the same thing is true of a number of the Jews in John's city. Perhaps for them, therefore, as well as for others, John translates the Hebrew title "Messiah."

But the important point to notice is that he is not satisfied merely to employ the translation alone. He emphatically uses the term itself, and he makes clear that he wants it to bear its full titular force.[130] This point may be grasped even more securely if one will read the whole of the section which extends from 1:35-51. Here we see that John is acquainted with non-Christian readers who already have conceptions of the Messiah. With *these* readers the task is not to awaken expectations of the Messiah, but rather—with certain qualifications—to announce that *Jesus* is the long-awaited Messiah. That is to say, 1:35-51 is not primarily designed to tell the reader that "Jesus is *Messiah*"; in the first instance it is composed for readers who already have (at least latent) expectations of the Messiah. To them John wants to say "*Jesus* is Messiah."[131] This fact must be kept in mind when one reads the perceptive comment of R. Schnackenburg.

It is remarkable how prominently featured in John is the question whether Jesus is "the Christ" (the Messiah). Indeed,

---

[130]Cf. W. C. van Unnik, "The Purpose of St. John's Gospel," pp. 167-96 in *The Gospels Reconsidered* (1960; selections from *Studia Evangelica, TU* 73); N. A. Dahl, "The Johannine Church and History," pp. 124-42 in W. Klassen and G. F. Snyder, eds., *Current Issues in New Testament Interpretation* (1962).

[131]A case can be made for the thesis that John 1:35-49 is composed on the basis of elements drawn from one of the homilies in which the messianic faith was first preached in the synagogues of John's city. See Martyn, "We Have Found Elijah," R. Hamerton-Kelly and R. Scroggs (eds.), *Jews, Greeks, and Christians, Essays in Honor of W. D. Davies* (1976), pp. 181-219; reprinted in Martyn, *The Gospel of John in Christian History* (1979).

all the more so in view of the fact that long before John wrote (already in Paul's writings) the expression Christ had become the name of the Christian redeemer. That use is attested in John itself in two places (1:17; 17:3, Jesus Christ); in all other instances, however [and there are 15 of them], the expression ο χριστος or χριστος (1:41; 9:22) is used to refer to the Jewish (or Samaritan, 4:25, 29) expectation of the salvation bringer.[132]

Thus, both for John and for his conversation partners in the synagogue, *the technical issue of Jesus' messiahship* is of paramount importance.

In closest connection with it stands another question: the correct interpretation of Jesus' signs. It is this issue which divides the Gerousia in John 9 (see particularly v. 16: How can a man who is a sinner do such signs?), and the same issue plays a similar role in John 7 (e.g., v. 31: When the Christ appears, will he do more signs than this man has done?). Indeed, we encounter here a leitmotif which, like the issue of Jesus' messiahship, extends far beyond the two dramas that have thus far claimed the major portion of our attention. One thinks immediately of the climactic sentence in which John states his purpose in writing the whole of the Gospel:

> Now Jesus did many other *signs* . . . which are not written in this book; but these are written that you may believe that Jesus is *the Christ* (ο χριστος). (20:30 f.)[133]

Four observations are necessary with regard to this statement. (1) The term "signs" is here used to refer to the whole of the Gospel. (2) It is equally important to say, however, that this is the only place in which John uses the term so broadly. In all of the other sixteen instances it refers in a relatively unsophisticated way to Jesus' miraculous deeds. He does signs by performing wonders. Thus, however broadly the term "sign" may be used in John 20:30 f., there too it includes the individual miracles related

---

[132]From p. 240 of "Die Messiasfrage im Johannesevangelium," pp. 240-64 in *Neutestamentliche Aufsätze* (Festschrift J. Schmid, 1963). See now Schnackenburg, *St. John,* p. 510.

[133]We shall see in a moment that the full text of 20:30 f. must be taken into account. For the time being the important term is "the Christ." See also the following note.

in the earlier part of the Gospel. (3) In his statement of purpose as in other passages to which we have just alluded, John uses the expression "the Christ" with its full titular force. One ought to translate 20:30 f. as it is given above, but with an awareness, gained from 1:41 and 4:25, that both John and his community are quite conscious of the equation: The Christ = The Messiah of Jewish expectation. (4) I do not mean to suggest, of course, that John recognizes in this equation an adequate statement of Jesus' identity. Such a suggestion would overlook the full text of 20:30 f., not to mention a host of other data which will shortly occupy us. John himself is not satisfied until he has said: ". . . but these are written that you may believe that Jesus is the Christ (o χριστος), the Son of God, and that believing, you may have life in his name." It is true nevertheless that, for John, Jesus' miraculous deeds witness to his identity as Messiah.[134]

Nor is this an opinion held only by John and his church. As John has portrayed them, members of the synagogue share this view.

> Yet many of the people believed in him, they said, "When the Christ appears, will he do more signs than this man has done?" (7:31)

Similar notes are struck at a number of points. For example:

> Now when he was in Jerusalem at the Passover feast, many believed in his name when they saw his signs which he did. (2:32)

> When the people saw the sign which he had done, they said, "This is indeed the prophet who is to come into the world!" (6:14)

Because the signs are so successful, causing the crowds to follow Jesus (6:2), to believe in him (11:45), to go out to greet him (12:18), and even to go away from the synagogue (12:11),[135] the Jewish authorities convene the Sanhedrin (Gerousia) to consider

---

[134]See Excursus E. If there was a Signs Document, its christological force must have rested on the assumption that a series of Jesus' signs (miracles) would, in fact, bear witness to his messianic status. Under what conditions such an assumption could be reasonably made in the first century is a question we will pursue in a moment.

[135]This is apparently the meaning of υπαγειν in 12:11.

a plan of action against Jesus, "For this man performs many signs. . . . Look, the world has gone after him" (11:47; 12:19).

It is true that John has definite reservations regarding "sign faith."[136] People who believe only on the basis of signs are not to be trusted (2:24), and their response is often inappropriate (6:15), for they have not really seen the signs (6:26). Dependence on signs is sharply rebuked (4:48; cf. 6:63 and 20:29). Indeed John can say that the signs have failed to awaken faith:

> Though he had done so many signs before them, yet they did not believe in him. (12:37)

But on two grounds we must not be deterred just now by these reservations. First, we will have ample opportunity to consider the fine nuances of John's own stance in our next chapter. And second, the very accent of failure which is expressed in the verse just quoted emphasizes the assumption that some, at least, should find in a recounting of Jesus' signs a significant indication of his messiahship.[137] Thus, to an extent recognized both by the separated church and by the synagogue, the Messiah is expected to be a miracle-worker. For this reason the technical question of Jesus' messiahship is decisvely bound up with the correct interpretation of his signs.

This seemingly innocent conclusion actually brings us face to face with a problem of some importance. Is there evidence to suggest that Jewish groups (or even one Jewish group) of the first century expected the Messiah to be a worker of miracles? In view of the importance which this question possesses for New Testament study, it is amazing that it has been largely ignored until recently.[138] Nor is it the case that the issue is so extremely complex as to invite neglect. The essentials may be briefly stated.

Jewish sources are not silent with regard to the Messiah. He is almost always expected to be the Son of David, since at its heart the messianic hope is patterned on the glorious period of Israel's

[136]Cf. R. T. Fortna, "Source and Redaction in the Fourth Gospel's Portrayal of Jesus' Signs," *JBL* 89 (1970), 151-66; and "Signs and Seeing in the Fourth Gospel," an unpublished paper by P. W. Meyer of Princeton Theological Seminary, Princeton, New Jersey.

[137]Important as 4:48 may be in John's whole view, it is equally important to note that of the seventeen instances of the term "sign" in the Gospel, 4:48 is the only clearly negative reference and the only one which links "sign" with "wonder," thus reproducing the ancient Hebrew expression.

[138]See now D. Moody Smith, "The Milieu of the Johannine Miracle Source," R. Hamerton-Kelly and R. Scroggs (eds.), *Jews, Greeks, and Christians* (1976), pp. 164-80, especially pp. 168 ff. and the literature cited there.

history under David.[139] He will, therefore, be a wondrous king who powerfully demolishes all bonds which hold Israel in subjection. Chapter 17 of the Psalms of Solomon, long held to be one of the most important sources for our knowledge of messianic hope, speaks of *the Messiah's works* (v. 40), and the context makes clear what these works are: the mighty defeat of Israel's enemies, the cleansing of Jerusalem from nations which oppress her, the gathering together of a holy people, the shepherding of the Lord's flock. For our present question it is of equal importance to point out what is *not* said regarding the Messiah's works. They are not said to include individual deeds which might be understood as miracles. Of course the Messiah is a wondrous warrior and a marvelously wise ruler. But he is not portrayed as one who heals the paralyzed, miraculously provides bread and water, restores sight to the blind, or raises the dead.[140]

Nor is the picture changed if we ask how the famous 35th chapter of Isaiah was interpreted in first-century Judaism. The pertinent text reads:

> Then the eyes of the blind will be opened,
> and the ears of the deaf will be unstopped.
> Then the lame man shall leap as a deer,
> and the tongue of the dumb shall sing.
> For in the wilderness waters shall break forth,
> and streams in the desert . . . (35:5 f.)

Here the prophet paints a picture of hope in which God will come with salvation. For while the verbs in the first two lines are passive, the context shows that the subject of the verbal action is understood to be God. Thus we have here—and other references could also be given—a portrait of a wondrous time characterized

---

[139]Strictly speaking, to refer to *the* messianic hope is somewhat misleading. First-century Judaism held its messianic hopes in a variety of patterns, directed, among others, toward Messiah ben David, Messiah ben Levi, Messiah ben Joseph, and Messiah ben Ephraim. See the standard texts on messianic hope, and particularly the very helpful dictionary articles by R. Meyer (*RGG*[3]) and E. Jenni (*IDB*); also A. S. van der Woude, *Die Messianischen Vorstellungen der Gemeinde von Qumran* (1957), where the messianic beliefs of Qumran are set in the context formed by other patterns. For our present purposes the statement may stand that the Son of David is the most frequently encountered messianic figure.

[140]Some of Jesus' signs in the Fourth Gospel are somewhat reminiscent of those attributed to Elijah, as we shall see below, note 172.

by miracles. The conclusion has been reasonably drawn that Judaism expected the messianic age to be a time of miracles. But since the Targum of Isaiah 35, like the original text itself, does not even mention the Messiah, this text is clearly inadmissable as evidence for an expectation of the Messiah as a miracle-worker.

There are a few references in Jewish literature to messianic pretenders who led crowds of people into the wilderness, promising the occurrence of signs.[141] But there is no indication that any of these men was thought to be the Messiah. Furthermore, the signs referred to appear Mosaic rather than Davidic; they are, so to speak, wilderness signs.

In the Tannaitic literature the situation is essentially the same.[142] To be sure, one will want to reckon with the dangers of drawing far-reaching conclusions from the Tannaitic references to the Messiah on two grounds: they are relatively few in number (not a single one in the *Mishnah*), and to some extent they may be influenced (negatively) by Christian messianism. Nevertheless it is important to note the categorical character of Klausner's statement.

> The Messiah—and this should be carefully noted—is never mentioned anywhere in the Tannaitic literature as a wonder-worker *per se*.[143]

---

[141]Josephus, *Bell.* II, 259; *Antiq.* XX, 167 f.; cf. *Antiq.* XX, 97. In the first of these references it is important to notice that the signs are (a) signs of deliverance (σημεια ελευθεριας), not miracles of healing, provision of food, etc., and (b) wonders to be performed by God, not by the messianic pretenders themselves. Essentially the same picture is given in the second reference. Theudas, mentioned in the third reference, promised to divide the Jordan River (the term σημειον is not used), but he represented himself not as the Messiah, but as a prophet. Careful study of these (and related) references will show, I think, that what calls for investigation in their case is in the first instance not the technical question of the Messiah, but rather the fascinating way in which the motifs represented by the terms πλανος and σημεια are interrelated. One suspects that behind this interrelation (cf. also Mark 13) lies Deut. 13; cf. the discussion of πλανος above, pp. 75 ff.

[142]Exceptions will be noted below, pp. 109 ff.

[143]J. Klausner, *The Messianic Idea in Israel* (trans. W. F. Stinespring, 1955), p. 506 (italics removed). That there are differences of opinion in regard to the rabbinic evidence must not be overlooked. Actually, the problem of a miracle-working *Messiah* arises not only in the Fourth Gospel, but also in Matthew. (Strictly speaking, it is absent in Mark, where the influence of the θειος ανηρ figure may be seen in both tradition and redaction.) Indeed, Matthew 12:23:

And all the people were amazed [at Jesus' healing of a blind and dumb

In light of the evidence, therefore, one can only blink when he finds Mowinckel speaking of "Messianic works and miracles."[144] And one's initial surprise is compounded when he notices that Mowinckel supports his point by referring to the data in John's Gospel with which we are presently concerned. These data present us, of course, with the problem, not with the answer! Thus one can scarcely say on the basis of *the Fourth Gospel:*

According to *Jewish thought* it is only then [when the Messiah openly performs what Mowinckel has just referred to as "the Messianic works and miracles"] that he will become Messiah in the full sense of the term.[145]

On the contrary. If Christian data be left aside, one will agree with the sweeping statement of Vielhauer.

N B In first-century Judaism the Messiah was not thought of as a worker of miracles.[146]

Nor is it surprising that a number of scholars have reached the same conclusion.

Though miracles were indeed a characteristic of the messianic period in Jewish belief, still the Messiah himself was not thought of as a miracle worker.[147]

---

demoniac], and said, "Can this be the Son of David?" sounds remarkably like John 7:31:
"When the Christ appears, will he do more signs than this man has done?" Commentators who sense the problem (they are exceptions!) usually point to *Pesikta Rabbati* 36 (162a), following Billerbeck, *Kommentar,* Vol. I, p. 641. But this appears to be the only reference of its kind, and it is a rather weak reed. It is late, and its real thrust has nothing to do with the Messiah's being a miracle-worker per se.
[144]S. Mowinckel, *He That Cometh* (trans. G. W. Anderson, 1951), p. 303. Mowinckel's book is extremely valuable on the whole.
[145]*Ibid.*
[146]Ph. Vielhauer, "Erwägungen zur Christologie des Markusevangeliums," pp. 155-69 in *Zeit und Geschichte,* ed. E. Dinkler (1964). The German clause is found on page 159: "Da im zeitgenössischen Judentum der Messias nicht als Wundertäter galt . . ."
[147]R. Bultmann, *Theology of the New Testament* (1951-55), Vol. I, p. 27. The same opinion is expressed by A. Schweitzer, *The Quest of the Historical Jesus* (1948). pp. 347 f.; F. Hahn, *Hoheitstitel,* p. 219; R. Fuller, *The Foundations of New Testament Christology* (1965), pp. 31, 192. Cf. further the standard works such as P. Volz, *Eschatologie,* pp. 173-86, 387 f.; Bousset and Gressman, *Religion,* pp. 222-30, 242 ff. In the same vein U. Wilckens comments helpfully on I Cor. 1:22 in *Weisheit und Torheit* (1959), p. 34, n. 1: "G. Stählin . . . rightly says that behind I Cor. 1:22 stands the assumption of a sensible revelation of the Messiah through signs; but he is unable to confirm this assumption *from Jewish sources"* (italics added).

Our problem is, therefore, a genuine one. John presupposes that his use of Jesus' miracles as evidence pointing to his messiahship will make sense to *Jews,* whereas Jewish sources seem to give us no reason to view this presupposition as a realistic one.[148]

In *general terms* a way out of our dilemma is not difficult to find. Jewish expectations of the future were extraordinarily varied. If it be true that there is no suggestion of miraculous activity on the part of *the Davidic Messiah,* it is equally true that the figures expected by Jews to play roles in the eschatological future (not only the various messiahs, but also the Son of Man, the Prophet like Moses, the Prophet like Elijah, and others) were allowed to coalesce in the most varied ways. Thus, while we must keep our problem firmly in mind—John does use the title "Messiah" in a careful, one might even say technical, way, as we have seen—it is just possible that traits "properly" belonging to another eschatological figure have "rubbed off" on the Johannine Messiah. We need to ask, therefore, whether the working of miracles is an activity properly expected of another of the eschatological figures. And, if that should prove to be the case, we must see whether the figure in question plays a role in the Johannine church-synagogue conversation.

A hint in this regard has already come to our attention. The passages in Josephus cited above in note 141 connect signs with the title "prophet," with the parting of the waters of a river, and with the wilderness. Obviously we must consider the possibility that the figure of Moses plays an important role in the Johannine church-synagogue conversation. It will suffice to cite a single reference from among the many which have already claimed our attention. In the course of their examination of the formerly blind man, the members of the Gerousia say:

> You are his disciple, but we are disciples of Moses. We know that God spoke to Moses, but as for this man, we do not know where he comes from. (9:28 f.)

---

[148]It should be clear that we are speaking of a problem which arises when a Christian seeks to support Jesus' messiahship in conversations with a non-Christian Jew. For a Christian to say to a fellow Christian that Jesus' signs witness to his messiahship is, of course, quite another matter. See M. de Jonge, "Jewish Expectations about the 'Messiah' according to the Fourth Gospel," *NTS* 19 (1972/73), 246-70, especially 258.

We may say, therefore, that the dialogue between John's church and the synagogue is punctuated by at least three issues, and the three may very well be closely interrelated: Is Jesus the Messiah of Jewish expectation? How is one correctly to interpret Jesus' signs? What is the relationship between Jesus and Moses? It may just be that the presence of this third issue explains to some degree the problematic relationship between the first two. In any case, since our interest is centered in these issues as they arise in John's church, we will look first at the role which Moses plays in John's Gospel. When we have a firm grasp on that, we may cast our net somewhat broadly in order to see if illuminating data are forthcoming from Jewish sources.

Part III

Major Theological Terms
of the Conversation

6

From the Expectation
of the Prophet-Messiah
Like Moses . . .

"As the first redeemer, so also the last."
"This is truly the Prophet."

We have seen that the Johannine church-synagogue conversation has at least three foci: the technical question of Jesus' messiahship; the correct interpretation of his signs; the relationship between him and the towering figure of Judaism, Moses. But we have only hinted at this third issue; we now need to look squarely at the data which pertain to it. The basic points present themselves when we pose two questions: What does each party to the conversation say about Moses? What does each say about the relationship between Moses and the Messiah?

1. Moses

As John portrays them the Jews are by no means silent with regard to Moses. They make affirmations about him in both explicit and implicit ways:

a. Explicit affirmations about Moses which the Evangelist attributes to the synagogue:
   1. "We know that god spoke to Moses." (9:29)
   2. "We are disciples of Moses." (9:28)
b. Implicit affirmations:
   3. Moses gave the Law to Israel. (7:19)
   4. The Law of Moses must not be broken. (7:23) For example, the sabbath must be strictly observed. (9:16; 5:10)

5. The Am ha-Aretz, who by definition do not know the Mosaic Law and who therefore do not observe it, stand under a curse. (7:49)

6. In contrast, those who are truly Jews diligently study ("search") the scriptures of Moses in the confidence of gaining life thereby. (5:39)

7. True confidence of gaining life by exegetical activity seems to rest on:

   a. a belief that in order to receive the Law, Moses ascended to God on Sinai; in his ascent he was granted a vision of heavenly things (note the polemic of 1:18; 3:13, 31-36);

   b. a conviction that by placing one's hope in Moses—by in fact believing in him (5:45 f.), i.e., by truly hearing the voice of Moses, the shepherd whom God commissioned for Israel (cf. 10:3)—one may oneself be granted heavenly visions (note the polemic of 3:3).[149]

It hardly needs to be said that John is not merely "reporting" the opinions of his Jewish neighbors. We need to ask, therefore, whether these seven affirmations are harmonious with what we know of Jewish theology from other sources. When we do so, we discover that every one of them can be found in Jewish texts which put us in touch with the first century. Beyond this it needs to be emphasized, however, that these seven points are not merely historically reliable. To a considerable degree they are representative of the very life nerve of Judaism, and they are stated in John's Gospel with great precision. Moses *is* the normatively authorized figure of Judaism. The Am ha-Aretz, who by definition do not know the Mosaic Law and who therefore do not observe it, stand under a curse.[150] We have good reason to believe that rabbinic scholars did refer to themselves as "Disciples of Moses," an expression preserved only by John

[149]I have drawn most of the aspects of this seventh point from the perceptive analysis of W. A. Meeks, *Prophet-King*, pp. 295 ff. Cf. also Meeks, "The Divine Agent and His Counterfeit in Philo and the Fourth Gospel," E. S. Fiorenza (ed.), *Aspects of Religious Propaganda in Judaism and Early Christianity* (1976), pp. 43-67.

[150]That Billerbeck assembled the rabbinic teaching regarding the Am ha-Aretz in his comment on John 7:49 is no accident. That verse (cf. 9:34) is the most transparently accurate reference to the Am ha-Aretz in the whole of the New Testament.

among early Christian authors, but attested also in rabbinic literature.[151] Such learned men did in fact "search the scriptures" (ερευναν = שׁדד), and they did so in the confident belief that "life" was to be found in the process.[152] Indeed in certain circles this "life" was connected with the affirmation of Moses' ascent to God on Sinai to receive a heavenly vision and with the personal hope for a similar gift.[153]

There is, then, nothing intrinsic to these seven points which indicates a distortion of the conversation. Quite the contrary. They stand proudly among the most accurate statements about Jewish thought in the whole of the New Testament. Furthermore, it is probable that John is ready to affirm a number of them himself. He clearly holds that God gave the Law through Moses (1:17). Because he believes that Moses wrote of Jesus (1:45; 5:39, 46), he might be somewhat patient *in his own way* with the expression "disciples of Moses." From a quite special point of view he would even agree that scripture (η γραφη, not ο νομος) has about it an imperative quality (cf. 7:23 with, eg., 20:9).[154] He may be less patient with the condemnation of the People of the Land; he clearly does not believe that life is to be found by studying the scriptures; and he stands strongly opposed to affirmations of ascent, the granting of heavenly visions, and divine commissioning for anyone except Jesus. In these seven points alone, therefore, we already see both agreement and tension.

2. Moses and the Messiah

The tension warms into debate at several points, two of which call for special attention. We have already noted one of these, the Jewish claims that Moses himself ascended on Sinai and was

---

[151] *Yoma* 4*a* (Billerbeck, *Kommentar*, Vol. II, p. 535; Dodd, *Interpretation*, p. 77 n.). Contrast Paul's expression "baptized into Moses," which is probably his own creation.

[152] It is a bit arbitrary to select one reference in Jewish literature to illustrate this belief. The whole structure of Jewish faith is built on it. It is important, however, to notice once more the accuracy of John's terminology. See the commentaries on John 5:39 and 7:52: ερευναν is the precise equivalent of שׁדד, the term from which the word "midrash" is derived.

[153] The primary data are collected and keenly interpreted in Meeks, *Prophet-King*, pp. 156 ff., 205 ff., 241 ff.

[154] As we shall see below, John provides us with data which make it possible to speak about the specific hermeneutic which he applies to the Old Testament.

granted visions, and the Johannine polemic directed toward these claims. We shall take account of this matter in the final chapter. The other point emerges when the discussion between John's church and the synagogue focuses not on affirmations or claims made about Moses himself, but rather on the relationship between Moses and the Messiah. Here, therefore, we must listen with special care. When we do so, we discover that this part of the conversation ranges over three central affirmations, the first two of which appear to be held in common by John's church and the synagogue:

a. In the Pentateuch Moses wrote of an eschatological figure whose coming is joyfully to be expected.

> Philip found Nathanael, and said to him, "We have found him of whom Moses in the law and also the prophets wrote." (1:45)

From the context in which this affirmation is made we learn that John believes this figure to be the Messiah (1:41; see also 5:46).

b. One of Moses' acts is to be understood as a typological prophecy of this coming eschatological figure.

> And just as Moses lifted up the serpent in the wilderness, so also must the Son of Man be lifted up. (3:14)

There is a formula for the relationship between Moses' act and an act done to the Coming One: "just as . . . so also."

c. For that reason, one may judge the authorization of a messianic or prophetic claimant by determining whether he "measures up" to Moses.

> So they said to him, "Then what sign do you do, that we may see, and believe you? What work do you perform? Our fathers ate the manna in the wilderness; as it is written, 'He gave them bread from heaven to eat.' " (6:30 f.)

Of course such measuring requires midrashic competence on the part of the ones making the judgment. But granted that competence, they may search the scriptures to see whether a claimant meets the requirements of the typology:

> They replied, "Are you from Galilee too? Search and you will see that the Prophet is not to rise from Galilee." (7:52)[155]

---

[155]I follow the reading of p[66] which has the article. See note 175 below.

The first two affirmations, as I said above, appear to be made by both parties to the conversation. It is the line which runs from the second to the third which reveals to us one of the major "rubs" between the conversation partners. Some kind of typological relationship between Moses and the Messiah is accepted by both parties. Just how this relationship is to be viewed is another question, and it is that question which now invites our attention. Before we delve more deeply into the Johannine text (sections 4 and 5 below), however, we ought to consider briefly the data given us in Jewish literature regarding Moses as a type either of the Messiah or of some other eschatological figure. Indeed the related question whether Moses is a type for the Prophet (John 6:14) or for the Messiah (John 7:31, 41; cf. Acts 3:17-26; 7:35 ff.) must be kept in mind.

3. Jewish Hopes for the Prophet or the Messiah Like Moses

By selecting eight brief texts from Jewish sources we can learn a great deal about the strands of eschatological hope gathered around Moses as a type of the coming redeemer.[156]

a. Moses speaks to Israel:

The Lord your God will raise up for you a prophet like me (כמני/ως εμε), from among you, from your brethren; to him you shall listen (אליו תשמעון/αυτου ακουσεσθε). (Deut. 18:15)

For God had said to Moses:

I will raise up for them a prophet like you (כמון/ωσπερ σε) from among their brethren; and I will put my words in his mouth, and he shall speak to them all that I command him. (Deut. 18:18)

However simply these verses may have been understood by their author,[157] they were destined to bear much fruit in later Jewish interpretation. In the post-exilic time, we may recall, the

---

[156]Cf. the very helpful appendix in Hahn, *Hoheitstitel*, pp. 351-404; also H. M. Teeple, *The Mosaic Eschatological Prophet* (1957), and T. F. Glasson, *Moses in the Fourth Gospel* (1963), but especially chapters II-VI in W. A. Meeks, *The Prophet-King*, a model of careful research.

[157]See, e.g., G. von Rad, *Old Testament Theology* (1962-65), Vol, I, pp. 99, 294 f.

line of prophets came to a close. In this period one hears the sad words:

> b. We do not see our signs (LXX σημεια); there is no longer any prophet, and there is none among us who knows how long. (Ps. 74:9)

Israel longed for a prophet not only because of generally dark times, but also because of specific problems. For example, in the Maccabean revolt the altar in Jerusalem was defiled with swine's blood. Upon taking the city, Judas was confronted with a difficult question. The stones of the altar were holy; yet they had been profaned. What should be done with them?

> c. And they pulled down the altar, and laid up the stones . . . until there should come a prophet to give an answer concerning them. (I Macc. 4:46; cf. 14:41)

Here we find, indeed, not only a longing but also a definite expectation. It is only a short step to a specifically eschatological interpretation of Deuteronomy 18:15, 18, and that step was taken prior to the first century C.E.

Among the scrolls of the Qumran community we now find two references which would seem to show the hope for a (the) prophet like Moses who is a definite eschatological figure distinct from the Messiah(s):

> d. They [the members of the community] shall be judged by the first regulations in which in the beginning the men of the community were instructed until the coming of a prophet and the Messiahs of Aaron and Israel. (1QS 9:10 f.)

One is reminded of 1 Macc. 4:46. It is confidently expected that a definite prophet shall come. That he is to be the Prophet *like Moses* is suggested in a remarkable collection of Old Testament quotations which would seem to attest the expectation of the same three eschatological figures mentioned in 1QS 9:10 f.:

> e. Ex. 20:21 (behind which stand Deut. 5:28 f. and 18:18 f.) referring to the Mosaic Prophet;
> Num. 24:15-17, referring to the Star of Jacob (=the Messiah of Israel);

Deut. 33:8-11, referring to the Priestly Messiah (=the Messiah of Aaron). (4Q Testimonia)[158]

Still other documents tell us that, however varied it may have been, there was a fairly widespread hope in Jewish thought of the first century for a figure whom we may accurately call the Prophet like Moses. Indeed, while it appears that for Qumran the Prophet is to be distinguished from the Messiah (or Messiahs), we must also recognize that in some circles the two figures coalesced to one degree or another.

f. The Samaritans, by rendering the Jewish ten commandments in nine parts, made room for a distinctly Samaritan tenth commandment which in its first part states "the vital dogmatic difference between Jews and Samaritans,"[159] the absolute sanctity of Mount Gerizim. A second part of their tenth commandment is, however, equally important. It includes the interpolation of Deuteronomy 18:15, 18. By granting to this promise so central a place, the Samaritans stated not only their claim for Mount Gerizim, but also their hope for a Redeemer like Moses (or perhaps, better expressed, Moses *redivivus*) whom they called the Taheb. Thus Gaster remarks:

Just as Moses brought the Law, so will the Taheb bring, as it were, the Law to the world, and just as the Israelites in the wilderness accepted it unquestioningly, so will they accept this text without further questioning.[160]

Just how the Samaritans of John's day formulated this Moses-Messiah typology we cannot say.[161] We can say that they

[158]J. M. Allegro, "Further Messianic References in Qumran Literature," *JBL*, 75 (1956), pp. 174-87, speaks of this as "Document IV." It contains four quotations arranged without intervening comments or formulae: the three canonical passages cited above and a quotation from another Qumran document, 4Q Psalms of Joshua. See J. A. Fitzmyer, " '4Q Testimonia' and the New Testament," *Theological Studies*, 18/4 (1967), pp. 513-37, and P. W. Skehan, "The Period of the Biblical Texts from Khirbet Qumran," *CBQ* 19 (1957), 435-40. That the texts are given in canonical order would not seem to exclude an interpretation linking them to three figures.
[159]Moses Gaster, *The Samaritans* (1925), p. 185.
[160]M. Gaster, *The Samaritan Oral Law and Ancient Traditions* (1932), Vol. I, p. 225. Cf. P. Volz, *Eschatologie*, p. 62; Bousset and Gressmann, *Religion*, pp. 224 ff.
[161]Note J. Jeremias' warning regarding Gaster's failure to give sufficient attention to the dates of his sources, *ThWNT*, Vol. IV, p. 867, n. 180. See now the

did so in dependence on Deuteronomy 18:15, 18.[162] The Samaritan Redeemer would repeat the great deeds of Moses, i.e., he would perform Mosaic *signs*.[163]

We may complete this brief statement by referring to the rabbinic data. Here the basic point to note is the maintenance of an ancient pattern which results from superimposing two (or all three) of the following:

Time of Creation
Time of Redemption (Exodus from Egypt)
Time of the End[164]

g. The earliest rabbinic passage explicitly referring to the Moses typology is attributed reliably to Rabbi Akiba (active C.E. 90–135).

How long do the days of the Messiah last? Rabbi Akiba said: Forty years. Just as the Israelites spent forty years in the wilderness, so will he [the Messiah] draw them forth and cause them to go in the wilderness and will make them eat leaves and straw. (*Tanchuma 'Ekeb* 7)[165]

And, while it is from a later date, a second reference is probably to be taken with equal seriousness.

h. Rabbi Berekiah said in the name of Rabbi Isaac: "As the first redeemer was, so shall the latter Redeemer be. What is stated of the former redeemer? And Moses took his wife and his sons, and set them upon an ass (Ex. IV, 20). Similarly will it be with the latter Redeemer, as it is stated, Lowly and riding upon an ass (Zech. IX, 9). As the former redeemer caused manna to descend, as it is stated, Behold, I will cause to rain bread from heaven for you (Ex. XVI, 4), so will the latter Redeemer cause manna to descend, as it is stated. May he be

---

work of J. Macdonald, *The Theology of the Samaritans* (1964), which is itself not entirely reliable, as W. Meeks shows in *The Prophet-King*, pp. 216-57 *passim*. Meek's treatment of the Samaritan traditions about Moses is quite illuminating, and may indicate that the statement I have made in the text is somewhat overly pessimistic.

[162] Also Num. 24:17 (Macdonald, *The Theology of the Samaritans*, p. 363). Cf. 4Q Testimonia cited above!

[163] Gaster, *The Samaritans*, p. 91.

[164] Most clearly thought through by II Isaiah. See the excellent treatment in von Rad, *Old Testament Theology* (1962-65), Vol. II, pp. 238 ff.

[165] Jeremias, *ThWNT*, Vol. IV, p. 865. Cf. Moore, *Judaism*, Vol. II, pp. 375 f.

as a rich cornfield in the land (Ps. LXXII, 16). As the former redeemer made a well to rise, so will the latter Redeemer bring up water, as it is stated, And a fountain shall come forth of the house of the Lord, and shall water the valley of Shittim. (Joel IV, 18) (*Qoheleth Rabba* 1, 8)[166]

Here the Moses-Messiah typology is set out in full clarity. While Rabbi Isaac (ca. C.E. 300) does not cite Deuteronomy 18:15, 18, we are probably correct in viewing his words as the full flowering of the influence which that passage exerted on Jewish thought in the first centuries of the common era.

Now we may gather the threads together. What do these eight references tell us?

1. While Deuteronomy 18:15, 18, was understood by the Deuteronomist to be a promise referring to an inexhaustable line of prophets rather than to an individual eschatological figure, it was interpreted in the latter way by various Jewish and Samaritan groups prior to the Christian era.

2. The oldest form of this interpretation appears to have referred the prophecy not to the Messiah, but rather to the Prophet like Moses. In the Qumran scrolls the Mosaic Prophet is apparently expected as a figure distinct from the Messiah(s).

3. However, both among Samaritans and among the rabbis a second step was taken. The Deuteronomic promise was understood to refer to the Messiah (or Taheb). We may call this a hope not for the Mosaic Prophet, but for the Mosaic Prophet-Messiah. There were, doubtless, a number of means at hand for expressing this hope. The most explicit was some such formula as כ . . . כן which is well grasped in Greek by the pattern καθως . . . ουτως, "just as . . . so also."[167]

4. In time—just how early is difficult to say—this typology acquired a certain degree of sophistication which we find in the second rabbinic quotation (*Qoheleth Rabba* 1, 8). The Moses-

[166]H. Freedman and M. Simon, eds., *Midrash Rabba*, 9 vols. (1939); Ecclesiastes is translated by A. Cohen, and the reference above is found on p. 33 of volume 8². Note that the expression "will . . . bring up water" renders the Hi'phil of עלה, i.e., "shall cause waters to gush forth." Cf. John 7:38.
[167]The comparative expression in the text of Deuteronomy itself is כמני which the LXX renders ως εμε. The rabbinic expressions are (1) כן . . . כ, (2) כן . . . מה, (3) אף . . . מה, all of which would be well rendered by καθως . . . ουτως or something similar. See Jastrow, *Dictionary*.

Messiah typology is there related to three specific signs: like Moses, the Messiah will ride upon a donkey, cause manna to descend, and cause waters to gush forth. While the rabbinic passages do not explicitly say so, it is easily imagined that the definite and sophisticated pattern expressed there could be used to measure possible claimants to the "office" of Mosaic Prophet-Messiah.

4. Opinions Among Synagogue Members in John's City

From this sketch one returns to the data in John's Gospel with new eyes. First of all, the problem which we brought with us from our preceding chapter—How can it be thought that Jesus' signs witness to his messiahship?—is placed in a new light. While it is true that the Davidic Messiah was not expected to perform signs, that is precisely what was expected of the Mosaic Prophet-Messiah. Indeed it may not be entirely accidental that John's is the only gospel which shows Jesus performing all three of the Mosaic signs mentioned in *Qoheleth Rabba:* he feeds the multitude (6:1-14); he quenches thirst (7:37 f.; cf. 4:13); he rides on a donkey (2:14).[168]

When we look at some of these references with care, we will have occasion to note John's distrust of the Moses-Messiah typology. For the moment it is enough to see that the middle term between the issues of Jesus' messiahship and the issue of correctly interpreting his signs may prove to be the step of identifying him as the Mosaic Prophet. We must now see whether that is, in fact, the case.

It would be foolish, of course, to claim a direct relationship between any of the Jewish sources we have briefly catalogued and the Jewish community in John's city. Whether some members of that community were formerly Essenes of the type

[168]I have said only that this congruence may not be entirely accidental, and the reasons for my reserve are obvious: the first and third of these signs were traditional in Christian circles very early. Furthermore Jesus' riding on the donkey does not seem to be understood by any of our Evangelists as a *Mosaic* sign. It is worth saying, nevertheless, that only in John's Gospel would a reader looking for the three signs of *Qoheleth Rabba* find them. John is also alone in explicitly interpreting the feeding as the repetition of the manna miracle and therefore as a transparent witness to Jesus as the Mosaic Prophet.

known to us from the Qumran scrolls cannot be said.[169] Whether in John's city there were flesh and blood Samaritans we cannot say with certainty, although it is quite possible that John 4 reflects the remarkable success of the Christian mission among Samaritans known to John.[170] What can be said is that in the Johannine synagogue there were many who knew well some form of the hope for the Prophet-Messiah like Moses who would perform signs. Indeed, we may proceed with reasonable probability to catalogue several shades of opinion in this regard.

a. Rank-and-file members.

There are six passages which seem to reflect at least in part the reactions of the common folk in the synagogue to the Johannine presentation of Jesus' signs.[171] Three of them show the hope for the Mosaic Prophet; three point to the Mosaic Prophet-Messiah:

6:14: This verse may have stood in a pre-Johannine source as the climax of the feeding of the 5000. The crowd understands this sign to be the repetition of *the manna miracle of Moses:* "When the people saw the sign which he had done, they said, 'This is indeed the prophet who is to come into the world.' "

7:40: It is scarcely chance that the second explicit confession of Jesus as the Mosaic Prophet comes on the heels of what is probably a reference to *the water miracle of Moses:* "Jesus stood up and proclaimed. . . . 'He who believes in me, as the scripture has said, Out of his heart shall flow rivers of living water.' . . . When they heard these words, some of the people said, 'This is indeed the prophet.' "

9:16 f.: This passage is by now familiar to us. The issue is how

[169]The questions usually asked are: Was John a former member of the Qumran sect? Does his work show direct literary dependence on Qumran literature? Or is there only a shared conceptual milieu? See the balanced treatment by Brown, *John,* LXII ff. If the line of argument we are following is correct, one must also ask whether there is some relationship between the thought patterns evident in the Jewish community of John's city and the thought patterns of Qumran. Cf. the essays collected in J. H. Charlesworth (ed.), *John and Qumran* (1972).
[170]See H. Leroy, *Rätsel und Missverständnis* (1968), pp. 92 ff.
[171]Here, as elsewhere in the present work, I have made a selection of the data to be presented. Through chap. 4 the criteria for that selective process were supplied by the *literary* observations that the dramatic sequences in John 9 and in John 5 and 7 correspond remarkably to the two prophecies made in John 16:2. These literary observations have led, in turn, to the positing of hypotheses regarding the Gospel's historical setting, and these hypotheses themselves now provide us with the major criteria for the selection of further data.

to interpret Jesus' sign of restoring the blind man's sight. Various opinions are offered: "Some of the Pharisees said, 'This man is not from God, for he does not keep the sabbath.' But others said, 'How can a man who is a sinner do such signs?' There was a division among them. So they again said to the blind man, 'What do you say about him, since he opened your eyes?' He said, 'He is a prophet.' "[172]

6:15: This verse may be John's addition to the traditional material in verse 14. It clearly bears theological weight in his picture (see below). Nevertheless it may also reflect the view of certain persons in the synagogue who proceeded beyond identifying Jesus as the Mosaic Prophet to the opinion that he is the Prophet-Messiah: "Perceiving that they were about to come and take him by force to make him King . . ."

7:31: Interpreters are commonly perplexed by this verse, for, as we have already emphasized, it is not characteristic of Jewish expectations of the Davidic Messiah that he should be a wonder-worker.[173] The problem is largely solved if we recognize the equation of the wonder-working Prophet with the Messiah: "Yet many of the people believed in him; they said, 'When the Christ appears, will he do more signs than this man has done?' "

7:40 ff.: Here we find essentially the same order of things as in 6:14-15. Interpreters often point to 7:40-41 as evidence that in John's Gospel the figures of the Mosaic Prophet and the Messiah are carefully distinguished from one another. In light of what we have seen, it is more likely that the passage reflects the easy

---

[172]Two factors may weaken the case for taking this passage as a reference to the Mosaic Prophet: the absence of the definite article and the fact that the sign is a miracle of healing. However, the absence of the definite article before the word "prophet" is by no means an infallible signal that the reference is to be taken in a general sense. See Hahn, *The Titles of Jesus in Christology* (1969), *ad rem.* And although we have no indication that Jews expected the Mosaic Prophet to be a healer, we cannot exclude that possibility. We do know that *Elijah* was revered not only as Israel's heavenly helper, but also as one who flew to earth to defend the righteous, to comfort the discouraged, and to heal the sick (Jeremias, *ThWNT,* Vol. II, pp. 932 f.). While Hahn is right to treat separately the hopes for the Mosaic Prophet and for a returning Elijah, we cannot assume such scientific precision on the part of first-century Jews, as Hahn himself realizes (p. 354). The possibility must be considered that in John's milieu the figure of the Mosaic Prophet has certain characteristics drawn from the hopes for the coming of Elijah. See Martyn, "We Have Found Elijah."

[173]See the generally unconvincing attempts of Dodd, *Interpretation,* pp. 89 f., and Bultmann, *Johannes,* p. 231, n. 5. Barrett, in his generally excellent commentary, passes by the main problem of the verse.

modulation from the Mosaic Prophet to the Mosaic Prophet-Messiah. Reading 7:40-43, one may see the following steps: (a) some say that Jesus' sign (the water miracle) shows him to be the Mosaic Prophet. (b) Others go further and conclude that he is the Mosaic Prophet-Messiah. (c) Still others say that the messianic conclusion cannot be drawn merely on the basis of the sign, since another factor must be taken into account: Messiah is descended from David and comes from Bethlehem. For the moment, step *c* does not concern us. The important point consists of the two confessions: Jesus is the Mosaic Prophet, Jesus is the Mosaic Prophet-Messiah.

For the most part one sees in these six references an unsophisticated, enthusiastic, and genuine response to Jesus' signs. These common folk are not technically trained theologians. They are rank-and-file Jews who, upon learning of Jesus' signs, immediately and uncritically view him as the Mosaic Prophet or Prophet-Messiah. They do so because of the pattern of thought we saw reflected in various Jewish sources; the problem which we have termed "the wonder-working Messiah" is for them no problem at all because of the typology which views the Mosaic Prophet as the middle term between Moses and the Messiah.

b. The Jamnia Loyalists.

When we see them in this light, the Jamnia Loyalists who dominate the Gerousia are not only reacting to the Jewish Christian threat by taking the disciplinary measures connected with excommunication and the beguiler charge. They are also taking a corresponding stance with regard to the theological question: Is Jesus the Mosaic Prophet-Messiah?

6:30 f.: If we recall the sophisticated kind of typology expressed in *Qoheleth Rabba* (pp. 109 f., above), we are not surprised to hear the demand being laid on Jesus that he prove his suitability for the "office" of Mosaic Prophet-Messiah.

> What sign do you do, that we may see and believe you? What work do you perform? Our fathers ate the manna in the wilderness; as it is written, "He gave them bread from Heaven to eat."[174]

---

[174]Those who speak are identified only as "the crowd." However, their expertise in midrash and the similarity between their argument and that of the Jamnia Loyalists in 7:52 (see below) lead one to conclude that in chapter 6 John portrays Jesus in conversation with that group.

7:40 ff.: See the reference to this passage above. In the series designated *a, b,* and *c,* it is evidently the Jamnia Loyalists, or laymen under their influence, who cite the scripture requirements of Davidic descent and Bethlehem birth as factors which preclude identifying Jesus as the Mosaic Prophet-Messiah. That is to say, they cite requirements for Davidic messiahship *against* a figure whom some are inclined to identify as the *Mosaic* Prophet-Messiah.

7:48, 52: We are here directly in touch with the Jamnia Loyalists. They interrogate their unsuccessful *Hazzanim:*

> Have any of the authorities or of the Pharisees believed in him? And don't cite to us the opinion of the common folk who are incompetent in midrash!

Furthermore they demand of Nicodemus:

> Search the scriptures and you will see that the Prophet is not to rise from Galilee.[175]

9:28 ff.: Finally, it is they who constitute the negative side of the schism in the Gerousia over the issue how the sign performed on the blind man is to be interpreted. Jesus is not the Prophet. Those who confess him as such (v. 17) have ceased to be disciples of Moses:

> You are his disciple. We are disciples of Moses. We know that God spoke to Moses, but as for this man, we don't know where he comes from.

What we find in these four references is the opinion of technically trained theologians. Their stance may be summarized in four points: (1) They affirm the Moses—Prophet/Messiah typology. It is part of their theological system. (2) But they deny that Jesus meets the requirements of this typology. (3) They insist that the question involved is a midrashic one, and (4) for that reason only scholars properly trained in midrash are competent to reach an

---

[175]Following the reading of p[66] which is almost certainly the earlier text at this point. See E. R. Smothers, "Two Readings in Papyrus Bodmer II," *HTR,* 51 (1958), pp. 109-11 and B. M. Metzger, *The Text of the New Testament* (1964), p. 40; contrast *The Greek New Testament,* eds. Aland, Black, Metzger, and Wikgren (1966), where the reading of p[66] is not mentioned. The Mosaic Prophet is to come, of course, not from Galilee, but from the wilderness.

authoritative conclusion. As we shall shortly see, the importance of the third and fourth points can scarcely be overemphasized.

c. The secret believers.

For obvious reasons members of this last group are more elusive than are the Jamnia Loyalists. But if we are correct in identifying Nicodemus as their representative, it is not impossible to suggest some lines characteristic of their thought:

12:42: In some sense they believe, but because of the dreaded threat of excommunication from the synagogue they do not openly confess their faith.

3:2: Nicodemus may represent both their faith and their fear when he secretly comes at night to examine the church's witness (N.B. 3:11 with its plural pronouns and verbs). The possibility that their secret faith is closely bound up with the hope for the Prophet like Moses is suggested by Nicodemus' somewhat cryptic confession. It may be a guarded reference to that figure:

We know that as teacher you have come from God; for no one can do these signs which you do unless God is with him.

It is on the basis of signs, the key characteristic of the Mosaic Prophet, that Nicodemus reaches his conclusion. To be sure, he uses the term "teacher" rather than "prophet." However, the Mosaic Prophet was expected not only as a wonder-worker but also as an authoritative teacher.[176] Moreover, and this is quite important, we may recall that when the Jamnia Loyalists rebuke Nicodemus, they do so in connection with the hope for the Prophet.

7:52: Indeed, they attribute to Nicodemus, without his objection, the opinion that Jesus is the Mosaic Prophet. The issue is whether his opinion can be midrashically defended:

[176]This very important facet of the hope for the Prophet finds its root, of course, in Moses' role as teacher and explicitly in the words of Deut. 18:15, "The Lord God will raise up for you a prophet like me from among you, from your brethren; *to him you shall listen*" (cf. John 10:20). The Qumran sect's *"Teacher of Righteousness"* may have been closely related to the Mosaic Prophet at some point in the history of the sect's thought (CD 6, 11). Similarly the Samaritans expected the Taheb as Mosaic Prophet and Teacher. Cf. also G. Bornkamm, "Der Paraklet im Johannesevangelium," pp. 12-35 in *Festschrift Rudolf Bultmann* (1949), especially p. 20, where Bornkamm remarks, "Die Vorstellung vom Messias als zweiten Moses bzw. als Prophet . . . scheint mir im Sinne von Dt. 18, 15.18 auch hinter dem Bekenntnis des Nikodemus zu stehen, Jesus sei ein von Gott gekommener Lehrer."

Search the scriptures and see that the Prophet is not to rise from Galilee.

From this verse one returns to the dialogue between Nicodemus and Jesus with the possibility in mind that Nicodemus' remarks are designed to secure data sufficient to mount a midrashic defense of his secret (and, to be sure, embryonic) faith. His opening statement may be, in effect, an invitation to a midrashic discussion of the implications of Jesus' signs; i.e., it may be a plea that Jesus provide further support which could be used by Nicodemus in a public defense of the view that Jesus is the Mosaic Prophet. The group of secret believers represented by Nicodemus agrees, therefore, with the Jamnia Loyalists that the issue of Jesus' possible identification as the Prophet is fundamentally midrashic in nature. They should like however, to avoid the choice posed by the Loyalists in 9:28; they should like to be disciples of Jesus who are able convincingly to quote Moses in support of that discipleship.

Apparently, therefore, we are able to identify with reasonable probability three attitudes represented in the Johannine synagogue. Bearing in mind the history of inner-synagogue discipline outlined above (pp. 64 ff.), we may suggest that the order of events with regard to the identification of Jesus as the Prophet was something like this:

1. In the theological treasury of the Jewish community in John's city was the hope for the Mosaic Prophet. Alongside it, or developing from it, was the expectation of the Mosaic Prophet-Messiah. In both instances a typology was presupposed like the ones we have seen in the Scrolls, the Samaritan Sources, and Rabbinic literature.

2. In the latter half of the first century some Christian Jews came into this community and persuaded a number of the synagogue members that Jesus was the Prophet-Messiah like Moses. One of these Christian Jews may have penned a collection of Jesus' signs to aid in the evangelistic effort. Among common members of the Jewish community—were they already influenced by followers of John the Baptist?[177]—such evangelization enjoyed considerable success, resulting in the emergence

---

[177]D. Moody Smith has recently revived and ably defended Bultmann's theory that the hypothetical Signs Source was directed to disciples of John the Baptist. See his article cited above in note 138.

of an inner-synagogue group of Christian Jews. Such success, however, brought official resistance. We have already explored the disciplinary measures introduced by the Jamnia Loyalists. They also mounted a theological attack, declaring the issue of Jesus' identification to be thoroughly midrashic and therefore off-limits to nontheologians.

3. These developments seem to have caused John to feel that the theology characteristic of his group during that early period was in certain regards inadequate for the new setting.[178] From the point of view of the Evangelist a crucial matter is the question how one is to respond to the secret believers among the theologians. These people, we may recall, are afraid to confess their faith in Jesus as the Prophet-Messiah unless they are assured of convincing midrashic grounds for defense. For they quite naturally agree with the Jamnia Loyalists that the issue must be settled by exegesis. Unless they can defend their secret faith on the basis of midrash, they feel they must choose between hiding their faith and being excommunicated.

5. John's Own Stance with Regard to the Mosaic Prophet-Messiah

At this juncture it will be helpful to consider the two major alternatives open to John. Confronted with conversation partners most of whom explicitly understand the issue to be midrashic in nature, he will probably have considered the possibility of accompanying them into the exegetical arena. By so doing he might convince larger numbers of the common folk, and he would provide the secret believers with what they understand to be their major need: powerful midrashic demonstration that Jesus fulfills the hope for the Prophet-Messiah like Moses. In an uncritical, unsophisticated way, that is apparently what his predecessor, the author of the Signs Gospel, did. In another locale it was the alternative selected by Matthew. And further removed, it was the route chosen by Justin. From the Qumran testimonia through early Christian collections of Old Testament texts to Justin and beyond, there stretches a line of thought which

[178]I have attempted a more complete picture of developments which seem to have taken place *between* the writing of the Signs Source and the authoring of the Gospel in "Source Criticism and *Religionsgeschichte* in the Fourth Gospel," D. G. Miller and D. Y. Hadidian (eds.), *Jesus and Man's Hope* (1970), I, 247-73; cf. also "Glimpses into the History of the Johannine Community."

accepts the burden of providing midrashic proof for messianic affirmations. This option was certainly open to John.

At the other extreme, he may have been aware of the possibility of abandoning altogether the christological implications of the Mosaic Prophet. It is perfectly obvious that a typological relationship between Moses and the Messiah was not viewed by every early Christian theologian as a necessary way of describing Jesus. Failure on John's part to enter the midrashic arena would probably close an important area of contact with members of the synagogue, but it is clear that the range of christological materials known to John was rich indeed. Other avenues less exegetically problematic could have been pursued.

Here we are struck by the remarkable polarity of John's thought.[179] Recall the technical formulae characteristic of the Moses-Prophet/Messiah typology:

כ . . . כן, etc.

καθως. . . . ουτως, etc.

And then notice two references which come, we may be sure, from John's own hand:

3:14 Just as (καθως) Moses lifted up the serpent in the wilderness, *so* (ουτως) must the Son of Man be lifted up.
6:58: This is the bread which came down from heaven, *not just as* (ου καθως) the fathers ate and died.

The first of these occurs in Jesus' conversation with Nicodemus, and, with minor reservations, we are bound to recognize it as the typological formula we have already studied. The reservations arise, of course, from the fact that instead of presenting Moses as a type for the prophet, it views an act of Moses as a type for an act which will be done *to the Son of Man.* Clearly John is very much at work here. We will shortly be concerned to explore the finer nuances of his stance. The point is that in 3:14 John employs the typological formula καθως . . . ουτως in a straightforward and *positive* statement about Moses and in the context of a discussion between two parties, one of whom is apparently seeking further data about the Moses-Messiah typology.

[179]Cf. C. K. Barrett, "The Dialectical Theology of St. John," pp. 49-69 in *New Testament Essays* (1972).

The other reference (6:58) stands as part of the discussion relating to the manna miracle of Moses, and it is just as clearly the *negation* of the typological formula: "*not* just as. . . ." Taken together, these two references define a problem with which we must wrestle. Where does John himself stand with regard to the Moses-Prophet/Messiah issue?

We must first of all entertain the possibility that his stance is somewhat flexible, that is to say that he expresses himself somewhat differently from time to time, depending on whether he has in view the laymen in the synagogue, the Jamnia Loyalists, or the secret believers, not to mention members of his own church.

a. John affirms that Jesus is the Prophet.

There are several indications that in some sense—which will become clearer as we proceed—John does affirm the identification of Jesus as the Prophet. The Samaritan woman is allowed to identify Jesus as a prophet (4:19), and in view of the fact that the Samaritans did not reverence the classical prophets, it is probable that the absence of the definite article is insignificant. In John's view she may be expressing an embryonic faith in Jesus as the Prophet. Further along she says,

> I know that Messiah is coming (he who is called Christ); when he comes, he will show us all things. (4:25)

Odeberg has suggested that the text orginally meant:

> I know that the Taheb is coming, he who is called Messiah.[180]

To this statement Jesus replies quite directly,

> I who speak to you am he.

We have already noted the clear and explicit way in which John's story of the miraculous feeding presents Jesus as the Mosaic Prophet (6:4, 14). And, finally we may recall that John allows the formerly blind man to confess Jesus as a (the) prophet (9:17).

Obviously, however, John is not formulating a concerted

[180]H. Odeberg, *The Fourth Gospel* (1929), p. 187; Bultmann, *Johannes*, p. 141, n. 5., renders his hypothetical signs source, "I know that the Taheb is coming, he who is called (by you Jews) the Messiah."

argument designed to show that Jesus is the Prophet. The finer nuances of his stance emerge as we realize that:

b. John denies to the Moses/Messiah typology any dogmatic force.

Consider once more Jesus' dialogue with Nicodemus.[181] I have already suggested that to a degree the dialogue reflects the quest on the part of secret believers in the synagogue for midrashic data sufficient to mount a defense of their faith. What is John's response? Notice how he handles Nicodemus' part of the conversation. It has often been said that Nicodemus is merely a foil who serves to set John's theology (expressed by Jesus) in bold relief. That is right as far as it goes, but the *transitions* from Nicodemus' remarks to those of Jesus show that there is more involved. For the transitions show a movement from Nicodemus' desire for midrashic discussion to Jesus' insistence on what may be called the dualism of election:[182]

1. An invitation to midrashic discussion: "Rabbi, we know . . . these signs . . ." (3:2)

   The issue cannot be understood as a need for further midrash. *The* question is that of election: "Truly, truly, I say to you, unless one is born anew, he cannot see the kingdom of God" (3:3)
2. Nicodemus wants to handle the question of rebirth in a rational manner: "How can a man be born when he is old?

[181]The separation of tradition from redaction in John 3 is extraordinarily difficult. I can say only that the elements with which we are presently concerned are, in the form in which they stand, very probably the work of the Evangelist. See K. Tsuchido, "The Composition of the Nicodemus Episode, John 2:23–3:21," *Annual of the Japanese Biblical Institute* 1 (1975), 91-103. The Nicodemus texts of John 3 constitute one of the points of contact between the Fourth Gospel and the "Secret Gospel of Mark," and were one convinced that the former is literarily dependent on the latter—or on a form of tradition accurately reflected in the latter—the task of separating tradition from redaction in those texts would be somewhat facilitated. But the case for such an assumption is quite problematic. See Morton Smith, *Clement of Alexandria and a Secret Gospel of Mark* (1973), *ad rem,* and R. E. Brown, "The Relation of 'The Secret Gospel of Mark' to the Fourth Gospel," *CBQ* 36 (1974), 466-85.

[182]Cf. J. H. Charlesworth, "A Critical Comparison of the Dualism in 1QS 3:13–4:26 and the 'Dualism' Contained in the Gospel of John," Charlesworth (ed.), *John and Qumran* (1972), pp. 76-106; and especially the keen observations of J. Becker, "Beobachtungen zum Dualismus im Johannesevangelium," *ZNW* 65 (1974), 71-87.

Can he enter a second time into his mother's womb and be born?" (3:4)

Jesus restates the issue as that of election: "Truly, truly, I say to you, unless one is born of water and the Spirit, he cannot enter the kingdom of God." Then he states the dualism which means, among other things, that midrashic discussion lies within the realm of human possibility and can never in itself lead beyond that realm: "That which is born of the flesh is flesh, and that which is born of the Spirit is spirit" (3:5).

3. Nicodemus continues to ask the "how" question: "How can this be?" (3:9)

In Jesus' reply the awesome dualism is concretized in the division of synagogue and church: "Are you the teacher of Israel and yet you do not understand this? Truly, truly I say to you, we [in the separated church] speak of what we know and bear witness to what we have seen, but you [in the synagogue] do not receive our testimony" (3:10 f.).

The same pattern of transition lies before us in John 6. We will look at it carefully in a moment. But first I want to mention another example which can be treated quite briefly. It is a clear instance of the Evangelist's choosing to reinterpret old Christian tradition in light of the plea for midrashic discussion which he hears from Jews in his own city.

7:15: "The Jews were offended at it [Jesus' teaching], saying, 'How is it that this man has learning, when he has never studied?' "[183] (cf. Mark 1:22; 6:2 ff.). The Jamnia Loyalists, in whose mouth John evidently places this sarcastic question (note 7:26), consider Jesus to be one of the Am ha-Aretz; certainly he did not study in a rabbinical school. How can *he* be an authority in midrash?

7:16 f.: Jesus' reply says forcefully that the issue is *not* midrashic, but rather one of decision dualism: "My teaching is not mine, but his who sent me; if any man's will is to do God's will, he will know in the moment of that decision (not via midrashic tests) whether the teaching is from God, or whether I speak on my own authority" (my paraphrase).

This instance of the transition pattern is so important as to call

---

[183]Bultmann and others are probably correct in taking θαυμαζειν here (and in 7:21) to mean "be offended at" rather than "marvel at."

for special comment. A rabbi does not speak on his own authority. He could, therefore, utter both the first and the last parts of Jesus' saying: "My teaching is not mine. . . . I do not speak on my own authority." The rabbi speaks, of course, on the authority of Moses. The force which his own words have, therefore, derives from his ability—gained from long study —correctly to interpret the writings of Moses.

It is clear that Jesus does not possess this kind of authority. Between the first and last parts of Jesus' saying lie words which emphatically exclaim: *The criterion of midrashic accuracy is wholly inapplicable to my teaching.* The issue is not midrashic, as both the Jamnia Loyalists and the secret believers suppose it to be. It is a decision of the will in the electing presence of God's emissary. One is not wholly surprised, then, to find that:

c. *John even formulates a negative Moses-Messiah typology in order to accent the motif of election in such a way as to show that the messianic question is not midrashic in nature.*

Here we must be especially careful to honor the sweep of John's thought in his treatment of the miraculous feeding sign. John 6 comes on the heels of the critical sermon in 5:19-47 which is designed (in part) to show the synagogue how the separated Jewish Christians can make a high christological claim for Jesus without abrogating monotheism. This theological concern matches the issue of the beguiler (one who leads others astray into an abrogation of monotheism), and that is the reason, of course, for John's placing the sermon immediately after 5:18.[184]

John 6 shows that the Evangelist has a related concern in mind, and a careful reading of the chapter will show what this concern is. For the whole of this complex literary piece is framed by the questions which indicate both the theme and some of its implications. They are Jesus' question to Philip (v. 5):

Whence are we to buy bread so that these people may eat?[185]

[184]A full analysis of John 5:19-47 would be appropriate here, but the demands of space preclude it. Notice the probability that v. 21 is an indirect, but for John's Jewish readers quite plain, reference to the Second Benediction in the *Shemoneh Esre* (Bauer, *Johannes,* p. 85). One of the major intentions of the sermon is "that all may honor the Son even as they honor the Father (v. 22 f.). It is therefore scarcely addressed solely to John's church.

[185]The kernel of the question is, of course, part of the tradition about the feeding of the crowd (Mark 6:37; 8:4 and parallels). But John shows that the initiative lies with Jesus, and by the following editorial comment (v. 6) he indicates the importance of the question.

and Peter's question to Jesus (v. 68):

Lord, to whom shall we go (for the bread/word of life)?

The theme of the chapter is "The Origin of Life," couched in terms of the tension between man's self-determination of his life and God's predestination to life. This theme is developed primarily, but not exclusively, with reference to the Eucharist, and in such a way as to make the connection between the Eucharist and predestination unmistakably clear. Basically, it is this connection which is so offensive both to the "the Jews" in the synagogue (vv. 41-59) and to "many of the disciples" in the church (vv. 60-71). Before we turn our attention to the specific question of the hope for the Mosaic Prophet-Messiah, it will be profitable for us to sketch the contents of the chapter in a way which honors this more basic theme. (The reader is asked to scan John 6 before proceeding.)

Note first the presence of four traditional elements: the feeding of the multitude (5-14); Jesus walking on the stormy sea (16-21); an argumentative statement regarding the earthly origin of Jesus (42*a* and *b*); and Peter's confession (68-69). The first two of these are combined in synoptic tradition; they may have come to John from a Signs Source. In any case we must carefully determine how John handles these traditional elements and how he forms his own lines of thought.

Verses 1-4: In his introduction the Evangelist strikes two notes: he informs his reader that a key issue is the interpretation of Jesus' signs and that the sign about to be narrated is to be interpreted against the background of the Passover. All that ensues is to be seen in light of that feast which celebrated Israel's redemption from Egypt under the leadership of Moses.

Verses 5-15: The traditional story of the feeding of the multitude is then presented as a sign. It is for John a sign in two important ways. First, it corresponds to the manna given through Moses. Jesus is therefore the Mosaic Prophet; John allows him to be explicitly identified as such (v. 14).[186] Secondly, John shows that he understands the feeding as a sign which points to God's gracious election (a Passover motif). We have already noted Jesus' question to Philip: "Whence are we to buy bread . . . ?" What is the origin of life? At the conclusion of the story, the same note is struck, but in negative terms: The crowd, having

[186]While vs. 14 may have come to John from his source, as suggested above, there is nothing in the narrative to indicate that John rejects this identification.

identified Jesus as the Mosaic Prophet, takes the additional step of viewing him as the King-Messiah. But they do this in a special way. They take it into their own hands to make Jesus king and thus show that they intend to preside over the question of the origin of life. John explicitly rejects this move. *God* elects men through Jesus, i.e., gives life through him.

Verses 16-21: In the traditional story about Jesus walking on the stormy sea, it is he who comes to his troubled disciples. He is the origin of life (N.B. v. 17).

Verses 26-71: With the stage set (via 22-25) for a full discussion of the feeding sign, John begins the dialogue in the Capernaum synagogue. Note the major steps: Continuing the motif struck in verse 15, Jesus perceives that the crowd has not seen the sign. Since they want to preside over the origin of life they are not willing to receive life as a gift (v. 27). Indeed, when Jesus challenges them to believe, they respond in the same vein. They intend to preside over the question by demanding a legitimizing sign.

> Then what sign do you do in order that we may see and believe in you? What work do you perform? Our fathers ate the manna in the wilderness; as it is written, "He gave them bread from heaven to eat."

It is important to notice that their demand is thoroughly orthodox. If Jesus is the Mosaic Prophet-Messiah as John has clearly implied (6:14), he should repeat the manna miracle according to the Moses/Messiah typology we have already discovered. One might accurately express the typology in these words:

καθως μωυσης εδωκεν αυτοις
αρτον εκ του ουρανου φαγειν
ουτως δωσει μεσσιας τον αρτον
εν τω αιωνι τω μελλοντι

Just as Moses gave them bread from heaven to eat,
so also will the Messiah give bread in the coming age.

But Jesus has just repeated this miracle! Clearly a subtle point is being driven home, and it is this: The crowd did not see the sign

(6:26). If they had, they would have recognized that as God's self-authenticating emissary Jesus presides over the issue of the origin of life with complete sovereignty. The point of the sign is not the Moses-Messiah typology but rather God's gracious election.

Therefore Jesus continues with a striking expression in which he places a negative immediately before Moses' name.

It was *not* Moses who gave you the bread from heaven; my father gives you the true bread from heaven. (v. 32)

Here we are in touch with the line of thought most important for our understanding of John's attitude to the hope for the Mosaic Prophet. We must weigh the words carefully. There is, first of all, a good possibility that in verse 32 John shows knowledge of a special Jewish method of exegesis helpfully illuminated by Peder Borgen. Notice the following elements:

1. The crowd quotes the Old Testament in such a way as to demand the Moses-Messiah typology, and that means, in all likelihood, that they understand Moses to be the subject of the verb "gave."

   Moses gave (εδωκεν/נתן) them bread from heaven to eat.

2. Jesus replies:
   Truly, truly I say to you
   Not (ου) Moses gave (δεδωκεν/נתן)
   to you bread from heaven
   but (αλλα) my Father gives (διδωσιν/נותן)
   to you the true bread from heaven.[187]

To a certain extent Jesus seems to be correcting the crowd's reading of the Old Testament quotation: "Not 'gave,' but 'gives.'" Borgen invites us to compare texts such as *Mekilta* on Exodus 16:15:

"Man did eat the bread of strong horses." (Ps. 78:25)
Do not read "of strong horses"

---

[187]P. Borgen, "Observations on the Midrashic Character of John 6," *ZNW*, 54 (1963), pp. 232-40 (cf. pp. 59 ff. in his book *Bread from Heaven*, 1965). Only in the final analysis do I think Borgen's suggestions are misleading, as I will indicate in a moment.

but "of the limbs,"
that is "bread" that is absorbed by the "limbs."
The examples which Borgen gives do seem to me to show that in John 6:31 f. the Evangelist is employing a midrashic method recognizable as such. They fail, however, to illuminate the main accent of his drama at this point (as Borgen partially realizes in his own way). Jesus is clearly doing much more than correcting the tense of the verb from "gave" to "gives." The emphatic negative by means of which he introduces his reply stands immediately before the word "Moses." And the subject of the second line is changed. The "correction" therefore is, "not Moses gave . . . , but my Father gives." John is strongly contrasting Moses with God!

That in itself shows us that the change of the verb tense is much more than a matter of midrash. The father of midrash is left behind, and one is brought face to face with the Father. John is not saying to the synagogue,[188] "You misread the text. You

[188]It is primarily with respect to the assumptions Borgen makes about John's addressees and purpose in writing (to refute Christian Docetists) that I find his work—otherwise so helpful—to be unconvincing. See the review in *JBL*, 86 (1967), pp. 44 f. The Johannine Epistles were not written, I think, by the author of the Fourth Gospel (cf. C. H. Dodd's Moffatt commentary). Nor were they directed to the same situation (cf. H. Conzelmann, "Was von Anfang war," pp. 194-201 in *Neutestamentliche Studien für Rudolf Bultmann*, 1957). Contrast also N. A. Dahl, "Der Erstgeborene Satans und der Vater des Teufels," pp. 70-84 (especially 80 f.) in *Apophoreta, Festschrift für Ernst Haenchen* (1964). Dahl speculates that Jewish gnostics, expelled from the synagogue through the Birkath ha-Minim, sought to attach themselves to the church. John is supposed to refer to them as "the Jews who had believed in him." But note the dependence on data in 1 John (p. 81, n. 39) which is taken to support the thesis that John 6 is antidocetic. I am more inclined to agree with Ernst Käsemann when he says that John himself *unconsciously* skirted rather close to *Docetic* thought forms (*Testament*, p. 26). But in the final analysis it is essential that we decide whether the Gospel is to be read as an entirely inner-church document. In *this* regard contrast Käsemann, *Testament*, a brilliant attempt to locate John's place in history by asking how his thought is related to other strains in early Christian thinking, with W. A. Meeks *The Prophet-King* and M. de Jonge, "Jewish Expectations about the 'Messiah' according to the Fourth Gospel," *NTS* 19 (1972/73), 246-70, which explore the Jewish background of John's Christology in very helpful ways. As far as I can see, the issue should be formulated in this manner: How are the aspects of the Fourth Gospel which reflect the church-synagogue tension related to the aspects which have primarily to do with inner-church concerns (in some texts Ἰουδαῖοι certainly do represent members of the church)? I do not see that the existence of either set of aspects can be convincingly denied. Recall again John 6:41 ("the Jews then murmured at him . . .") and John 6:60 ("many of his disciples, when they heard it, said . . ."), not to mention other texts. See Martyn, "Glimpses Into the History of the Johannine Community"; also the studies by G. Richter and R. E. Brown cited above in note 84.

should read it, 'He *gives* them bread from heaven to eat.' "
Rather he is emphatically saying:

1. "You are wrong in your identification of the type. It was not Moses but rather God who provided the manna." From this affirmation we may perhaps conclude that for John typological thought must show God to be the subject in both type and antitype, or in neither.

2. "The correspondence between type and antitype is fixed by God in his sovereign freedom." Thus, the essential line extends not from type to antitype

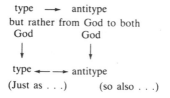

```
        type  ——►  antitype
     but rather from God to both
        God          God
         |            |
         ▼            ▼
        type ◄—— ——► antitype
     (Just as . . .)    (so also . . .)
```

From this it is apparent that one may see a typological relationship only after he has been grasped by God in the second member of it, never before being so grasped.[189]

3. "The issue is not to be defined as an argument about an ancient text. It is not a midrashic issue. By arguing about texts you seek to evade the present crisis. God is *even now* giving you the true bread from heaven, and you cannot hide from him in typological speculation or in any other kind of midrashic activity. You must decide now with regard to this present gift of God."

In short, by having Jesus speak in the present tense

. . . my Father *gives* . . .

I am the bread of life

John allows Jesus paradoxically to employ a form of midrashic discussion in order to terminate all midrashic discussion! Far from being predicated on certain exegetical patterns such as the Moses-Messiah typology, faith has only one essential presupposition: the presence of Jesus and his self-authenticating word,

I am the bread of life.

[189]Cf. D. Bonhoeffer, *Ethics* (1955), pp. 91 ff.: "What is this penultimate? It is everything that precedes the ultimate, . . . everything which is to be regarded as leading up to the last thing *when* the last thing has been found. . . . a thing becomes penultimate only through the ultimate" (italics added). In the new edition (1965) see pp. 133 ff.

7

... to the Presence of
the Son of Man

*"Do not labor for the food which perishes, but for the food which endures
to eternal life, which the Son of Man will give to you."*
*"It was not Moses who gave you the bread from heaven; . . . I am the
bread of life."*

1. The Two-Level Drama

Theologically the boldest step we have seen John take is the
"doubling" of Jesus with the figures of Christian witnesses in his
own community. Since we are acquainted with Luke's second
volume in which a part of the post-resurrection history of the
church is narrated, it strikes us that John could have narrated the
history of his own church in a direct and straightforward manner.
Instead, we find him presenting a two-level drama in which it is
not an apostle but rather Jesus himself who ministers to Jews
known to John as men who have suffered the fate of
excommunication from the synagogue. Jesus also acts the part of
the Jewish-Christian preacher who is subjected to arrest and trial
as a beguiler. Jesus engages in the debates which John's church
has with the Jewish community regarding his own identity as the
Mosaic Messiah. It is also the Risen Lord himself who insists that
the messianic issue is not midrashic and who terminates these
debates with his awesome use of the numinous-laden "I am." It is
now time for us to face squarely the christological problems
which are posed by this two-level drama.

At first glance it might seem that the Christology of the drama
is a rather "low" one. If the part of Jesus can be acted on the
contemporary level by persons in John's church, then the
church's Lord would scarcely appear to be an unapproachable
figure who dwells outside the world of men. On the other hand,

129

one might say that the Christology of the two-level drama, like that of John's Gospel as a whole, is quite "high," and that it is precisely the movement from the *einmalig* level of the drama to its contemporary level which makes it so. Jesus' identity is not an issue which can be decided by asking who he was. Quite the contrary. He is *present,* and he makes his presence known by pronouncing an extremely high christological claim: "I am the bread of life . . . come down from heaven" (6:35, 38). It may be that our terms "low" and "high" are simply not exegetical with regard to John's Gospel. As the Evangelist expands pieces of *einmalig* tradition into two-level dramas, he produces what we may call a dynamic christological *movement* portrayed in a story about (a) Jesus of Nazareth who (b) in John's own day identifies himself with flesh-and-blood Christian witnesses and yet claims solemnly to be the Son of God.

2. Mosaic Messiah and Son of Man

A second line of christological movement closely related to that of the two-level drama emerges when we pursue further than we did in the preceding chapter John's attitude toward the identification of Jesus as the Mosaic Messiah. We have already seen that John's stand on this question is neither a simple affirmation of the typology nor a simple denial of it. On the contrary, he has worked out a sophisticated position on this issue, as on others. He evidently considers the identification of Jesus as the Mosaic Messiah to be a legitimate stage in the growth of faith. To be sure, this identification is nothing less than the kiss of death (6:27, 36) if it is employed as a call to midrashic discussion on the basis of which man will decide whether God's bread of life is present or not. The issue is not a matter of better exegesis but rather of election. On the other hand, John does consider Jesus to be the Mosaic Messiah. Moses wrote of him (5:46; perhaps a reference to Deut. 18:15, 18). Moses' acts are typological prophecies of Jesus (3:14; 7:38-40). It seems clear that John wants to lead the common folk from a confession of Jesus as the Prophet–Messiah to a faith which he considers more adequate. When we reconsider the data which claimed our attention in the preceding chapter, we see to a certain extent what this more adequate faith is.

The church-synagogue conversations which reflect an interest in the figure of the Mosaic Prophet–Messiah have left their mark in a major way on four passages in our Gospel: (1) Jesus' conversation with Nicodemus (3:1 ff.); (2) the miraculous feeding sign and the ensuing dialogue (6:1 ff.); (3) the near-arrest of Jesus as he teaches in the Temple (7:25 ff.); and (4) the drama about the man born blind (9:1 ff).[190] When we ask whether there is a pattern of christological movement involving the Prophet, we are struck with data which may be presented in the form of a chart:

Jesus as the Mosaic Prophet–Messiah	A midrashic discussion of that identification	Jesus as the Son of Man

1. Jesus' conversation with Nicodemus

a. Rabbi, we know that you are a teacher come from God; for no one can do these signs that you do, unless God is with him. (3:2)		
	b. How can a man be born when he is old? Can he enter a second time into his mother's womb and be born? (3:4; cf. 3:9)	
		c. No one has ascended into heaven but he who descended from heaven, the Son of Man. (3:13)[191]

[190] I leave aside the Samaritan episode (4:4 ff.) which does not reflect discussion with the synagogue. John's polemic against Jewish claims that Moses himself ascended and was granted visions will emerge as we proceed. For detailed treatment of this subject see Meeks, *Prophet-King,* pp. 297 ff. and three articles by Meeks, "The Man from Heaven in Johannine Sectarianism," *JBL* 91 (1972), 44-72; " 'Am I a Jew?' Johannine Christianity and Judaism," J. Neusner (ed.), *Christianity, Judaism, and Other Greco-Roman Cults* (1975), I, 163-86; "The Divine Agent and His Counterfeit in Philo and the Fourth Gospel," E. S. Fiorenza (ed.), *Aspects of Religious Propaganda in Judaism and Early Christianity* (1976), pp. 43-67.

[191] This verse is surely polemical with respect to claims being made as regards Moses' ascent and visions (cf. 1:18), and its polemical nature makes the christological movement doubly clear. Cf. S. Schulz, *Menschensohn-Christologie,* p. 106, n. 3; W. A. Meeks, *The Prophet-King,* pp. 122 ff., 156 ff., 241 ff., and especially 297 ff.

Jesus as the Mosaic Prophet–Messiah	A midrashic discussion of that identification	Jesus as the Son of Man
d. As Moses lifted up the serpent in the wilderness,		
		e. So must the Son of Man be lifted up. (3:14)

2. The miraculous feeding sign and ensuing dialogue

a. When the people saw the sign which he had done, they said, "This is indeed the prophet who is to come into the world. (6:14)		
	b. So they said to him, "Then what sign do you do, that we may see, and believe you? What work do you perform? Our fathers ate the manna in the wilderness; as it is written, He gave them bread from heaven to eat." (6:30 f.)	
		c. Jesus said to them, "I am the bread of life . . . I have come down from heaven. . . . Truly, truly, I say to you, unless you eat the flesh of the Son of Man and drink his blood, you have no life in you." (6:35, 38, 53; cf. 6:27)[192]

3. The near-arrest of Jesus as he teaches in the Temple

a. Yet many of the people believed in him; they said, "When the Christ appears, will he do more signs than this man has done?" . . . "This is really the prophet." (7:31, 40)		

[192]Perhaps one should identify two transitions of this sort in John 6. The stage is set by the Moses-Messiah typology (v. 14). Jesus' speech, however, is introduced by a reference to the Son of Man (v. 27).

132

Jesus as the Mosaic Prophet–Messiah	A midrashic discussion of that identification	Jesus as the Son of Man
	b. They replied, "Are you from Galilee too? Search and you will see that the prophet is not to rise from Galilee." (7:52; cf. 7:42; 8:13)	
		c. Again Jesus spoke to them, saying, "I am the light of the world. . . . When you have lifted up the Son of Man, then you will know that I am he . . ." (8:12, 28)

4. The drama of the man born blind

a. So they again said to the blind man, "What do you say about him, since he opened your eyes?" He said, "He is a [the] prophet." (9:17)		
	b. And they reviled him, saying, "You are his disciple, but we are disciples of Moses. We know that God has spoken to Moses, but as for this man, we do not know where he comes from. . . . You were born in utter sin, and would you teach us?" (9:28 f., 34)	
		c. Jesus heard that they had cast him out, and having found him he said, "Do you believe in the Son of Man?" He answered, "And who is he, sir, that I may believe in him?" Jesus said to him, "You have seen him, and it is he who speaks to you." He said, "Lord, I believe"; and he worshiped him. (9:35 ff.)

133

From this chart we see that John never allows the identification of Jesus as Mosaic Prophet–Messiah to occupy center stage without causing it shortly thereafter to be replaced by another motif. Furthermore, this other motif always has to do with the Son of Man,[193] and it usually consists of a direct presentation of Jesus as the Son of Man.[194] Beyond the negative point of John's categorical denial that the messianic issue is midrashic lies his positive concern to lead his reader to a direct confrontation with Jesus as the Son of Man.[195]

If anyone doubts that this patterned movement from the Prophet to the Son of Man is John's own creation, a careful reading of 3:14 will probably convince him that it is. We see the precise terminology of the typological relationship: καθως . . . ουτως, and the first term of the relationship is an act of Moses. That will certainly have prepared many readers to find as the second term the Prophet or the Prophet-Messiah, and there is no doubt that the configuration does place in a typological relationship with one another an act connected with the first redeemer and an act connected with the last redeemer. But all of

[193]We are here in touch with the fact—so puzzling to W. Bousset and others who placed John's Gospel solidly in the history of the Gentile, Hellenistic church after the impact of Paul—that the Jewish Christian title "Son of Man" occupies center stage in John's Christology. It is true, as R. E. Brown pointed out in a review of the first edition of the present work (*USQR* 23 [1968], 394), that the Evangelist himself states the purpose of his writing to be "that you may believe that Jesus is the Christ, the Son of *God.*" (20:31). But the titles Son of Man and Son of God have become interchangeable for John, as S. Schulz has shown in *Menschensohn-Christologie,* and the passages which demonstrate the centrality of the title Son of Man far outweigh those which emphasize the other title. See note 195 below.

[194]Again the single exception is the Samaritan episode in John 4. There, appropriately, the movement is from the Mosaic Taheb to the Jewish Messiah to the Savior of the World.

[195]The christological movement from the identification of Jesus as the Mosaic Prophet–Messiah to the confession of him as Son of Man poses fascinating problems as regards John's place in the history of early Christianity. That the early and decidedly Jewish stages of the community's thought should be focused on Jesus as the Mosaic Prophet–Messiah is no cause for surprise (cf. R. H. Fuller, *The Foundations of New Testament Christology* [1965] *ad rem*). But if we are to think of the completed Gospel as reflecting, in its own way (shades of F. C. Baur), developments toward the emergence of the Great (essentially Gentile) Church, then an emphasis on confessing Jesus as the Son of Man is curious, to say the least. See the studies by Martyn, Richter, and Brown cited above in note 84; also U. B. Müller, *Die Geschichte der Christologie in der Johanneischen Gemeinde* (1975).

this only emphasizes the fact that as the second term John mentions neither the Prophet nor the Messiah, but rather the Son of Man. In doing so he does not create *ex nihilo,* of course. There is old Christian tradition for the necessity (δει) of the Son of Man's death (Mark 8:31, etc.). But just as the verb "lift up" is here used in its peculiarly Johannine way, so the unexpected movement from Moses to the Son of Man is John's own creation.[196]

When we recall the probability that the source from which John took his miracle-story tradition found its theological center in the christological affirmation that Jesus was the Mosaic Prophet–Messiah, we can peer over John's shoulder and see that, in order to achieve that part of his own Christology which presently concerns us, he takes two major steps. In the first place he creates from the *einmalig* tradition about Jesus of Nazareth a two-level drama which shows Jesus to be *present* in the activity of the Christian witness. Second, while John demonstrates an interest in the figure of the Mosaic Messiah, he insists that Jesus makes his presence unmistakably clear not as the Mosaic Messiah, but as the Son of Man on earth. We will grasp the implications of these two moves on John's part much more adequately if we consider comparable phenomena in other literature.

3. The Two-Level Drama and the Son of Man in Other Literature

John did not create the literary form of the two-level drama. It was at home in the thought-world of Jewish apocalypticism. The dicta most basic to the apocalyptic thinker are these: God created both heaven and earth. There are dramas taking place both on the heavenly stage and on the earthly stage. Yet these dramas are

---

[196]There is one other place in the New Testament at which one encounters a kind of movement from the Mosaic Prophet to the Son of Man: Acts 7. Stephen's speech is in part a midrash on the Mosaic typology, whereas the climax of this first Christian martyrdom finds Stephen gazing into heaven where he beholds the Son of Man. So far as I can see, however, there is little to indicate any significant connection between Acts 7 and the pattern we are investigating in John's Gospel. If interpreters are correct who link the verb ατενιζειν in Acts 6:15 with the same verb in 7:55, considering the intervening verses to be Luke's insertion into a pre-Lucan piece of tradition, then it is Luke himself who caused the juxtaposition of the Prophet-theology and the vision of the Son of Man. But I doubt that he was conscious of constructing a "pattern." As Luke portrays the expansion of the church, he has little interest in the title "Son of Man."

not really two, but rather one drama. For there are corresponding pairs of actors; a beast of a certain description in heaven represents a tyrannical king on earth, etc. Furthermore, the developments in the drama on its heavenly stage determine the developments on the earthly stage. One might say that events on the heavenly stage not only correspond to events on the earthly stage, but also slightly precede them in time, leading them into existence, so to speak. What transpires on the heavenly stage is often called "things to come." For that reason events seen on the earthly stage are entirely enigmatic to one who sees only the earthly stage. Stereoptic vision is necessary,[197] and it is precisely stereoptic vision which causes a man to write an apocalypse:

> After this I looked, and lo, in heaven an *open door*! And the first voice which I had heard . . . said, Come hither, and I will show you what must take place after this." (Rev. 4:1)

When we turn again to John's two-level drama, three changes are immediately apparent. (1) Both of his stages are on earth. To be sure, he has much to say about the "above" and the "below." Since Jesus is "from above," the world is to him foreign territory, even though he was the mediator of creation. He tries in vain to instruct Nicodemus about "heavenly things." Jesus comes from the Father and returns to the Father. But the fact remains that both the *einmalig* tradition and John's extension of it into the contemporary level of his drama portray events in the world.[198]

(2) Furthermore, John handles the temporal distinction between the two stages in a way quite different from that which is characteristic of Jewish apocalyptic. The initial stage is not the scene of "things to come" in heaven. It is the scene of Jesus' life and teaching. Its extension into the contemporary level "speaks to" current events not by portraying the immediate future, but by narrating a story which, on the face of it, is about the past, a story

[197]Apocalyptic thought therefore carries with itself profound epistemological implications. This fact stands behind many motifs in early Christian thought, such as the famous Messianic Secret in Mark. Regarding the epistemological crisis which John believes to be effected in Jesus' coming, see Martyn, "Source Criticism and *Religionsgeschichte* in the Fourth Gospel," especially p. 257, and Meeks, "Man From Heaven," especially pp. 54 and 57.

[198]John writes a gospel, not an apocalypse, but the relation of his Gospel to the Apocalypse should probably be re-examined in light of the way in which he presents his two levels.

about Jesus of Nazareth.[199] We will consider in a moment the highly important passage in which John allows Jesus to mention "things to come." For the present it will suffice to say that the reference is not to events transpiring on a future, heavenly stage which determine events on an earthly, present stage. John's two stages are past and present, not future and present.

(3) The third change lies before us in the fact that John does not in any overt way indicate to his reader a distinction between the two stages.[200] He speaks neither of heavenly visions which demand interpretation nor of open doors through which one may pass to heaven in order to see the other level of the drama. Indeed, we must say the very opposite. He presents his two-level drama in a way which is obviously intended to say with emphasis: "This is *the* drama of life." Only the reflective scholar intent on *analyzing* the Gospel will discover the seams which the Evangelist sewed together so deftly. True exegesis demands, therefore, that we recognize a certain tension between our analysis and John's intentions.

I have indicated above that the christological movement from the Mosaic Messiah to the Son of Man is John's own creation. Strictly speaking, therefore, we cannot place it alongside a comparable phenomenon in other literature. But the climactic term of this christological movement, the Son of Man, is even better known to us from the literature of the first century than is the first term; and we will grasp more clearly what John intends by this line of movement if we compare his Son of Man with that figure as he is presented elsewhere.

The figure of the Son of Man, like the phenomenon of the two-level drama, is originally at home in apocalyptic thought.[201] We cannot say that the picture of him which we receive from apocalyptic literature is always and everywhere presented in the

---

[199]That is a development with which the synoptic evangelists were certainly acquainted (e.g., problems of discipline in the Christian community, Matt. 18:15 ff.; the destruction of Jerusalem in A.D. 70, Matt. 22:7). Indeed it belongs to the very nature of the genre "gospel" to present in some degree a two-level drama; but none of the Synoptists created a two-level drama of the precise sort we have found in John's Gospel.

[200]See the comments above, pp. 88 f.

[201]I do not mean to express an opinion regarding the ultimate origin of the figure. See the works of Rost, Morgenstern, and Colpe referred to in N. Perrin, *Rediscovering the Teaching of Jesus* (1967), p. 166, n. 1.

same way, but if we take our main cue from Daniel 7, his primary features are relatively constant.[202] The Son of Man is a figure whose proper locale is heaven. He acts, therefore, "in a transcendent place rather than within the boundaries of the existing world."[203] The author of Daniel portrays a heavenly figure "like a son of man" to whom God grants awesome authority:

> And to him was given dominion (LXX, εξουσια) and glory and kingdom, that all peoples, nations and languages should serve him; his dominion is an everlasting dominion, which shall not pass away, and his kingdom one that shall not be destroyed. (Dan. 7:14)

Later writers, depending on Daniel, speak of the Son of Man who is empowered by God to be the cosmic judge at the end of time. God appoints him to annihilate the sinners and to lead those who are elect and righteous to a supraterrestrial salvation.[204] The author of I Enoch 62 paints a picture of heaven at the end of time when he shows the separation of the righteous from the sinners:

> And the righteous and elect shall be saved on that day,
> And they shall never thenceforth see the face of the sinners and unrighteous.
> And the Lord of Spirits will abide over them,
> And with that Son of Man shall they eat
> And lie down and rise up for ever and ever.

The Son of Man is, therefore, not only a figure of heaven, but also a figure of judgment and of the future. His activity will mark

[202]The primary features remain *relatively* constant for the simple reason that, by and large, the motifs of Daniel 7 impregnate all of the Son of Man traditions. It is essential to note that this fact is taken quite seriously by N. Perrin, who has suggested the absence of a Son of Man concept in Judaism in *Rediscovering the Teaching of Jesus*, pp. 164 ff., 260. For our purpose the presence or absence of a Son of Man *concept* in Judaism is of no great consequence. The *profile* of the one like a Son of Man in Daniel 7 indicates him to be a cosmic judge who acts in a transcendent realm. These two features remain, as I said above, relatively constant, and it is only these two features (not the Son of Man's "coming," etc.) which interest us.
[203]H. E. Tödt, *The Son of Man,* p. 29.
[204]*Ibid.*

the cosmic, catastrophic *krisis* which terminates the earthly course of events.

The way in which John presents Jesus as the Son of Man shows both continuity and discontinuity with this "traditional" picture. For John, the Son of Man has authority, just as does the one like a son of man in Daniel:

(a) John 5:27a: και εξουσιαν εδωκεν αυτω . . .
  Dan. 7:14: και εδοθη αυτω εξουσια
(b) John 5:27b: . . . υιος ανθρωπου
  Dan. 7:13: . . . υιος ανθρωπου[205]

His authority, furthermore, is explicitly that of the judge, and this authority has been handed over to him by God, as the same verse tells us:

And he [God] has given to him authority to execute judgment because he is the Son of Man. (5:27)

We are reminded not only of Daniel 7:13 f., but also of Enoch 69:27:

And he sat on the throne of his glory, and the sum of judgment was given to the Son of Man, and he caused the sinners to pass away and be destroyed from off the face of the earth.[206]

In some respects John 5:27 appears to be the most "traditional" Son of Man saying in the whole of the New Testament.

The Evangelist has some surprises in store, however, in the remaining eleven references to the Son of Man. He binds the Son of Man to Old Testament figures (Jacob/Israel in 1:51; Moses in 3:12),[207] to the motif of a descending and ascending redeemer (3:13 and 6:62), to the language of sacramental mystery (6:27 and 6:53), and to two verbs on which he lays considerable weight: "to lift up," and "to glorify" (3:14; 8:28; 12:34; and 12:23; 13:31). And, finally, he allows Jesus to draw from the man born blind a confession of him as the Son of Man (9:35 ff.).[208]

[205]S. Schulz, *Menschensohn-Christologie*, p. 111. Note the anarthrous state in each case.
[206]*Ibid.*, p. 112, n. 5.
[207]This is not surprising in itself, of course.
[208]Cf. Schulz, *Komposition*, p. 133, who allots, however, to pre-Johannine tradition far too much of the creativity displayed in this combining of the Son of Man with motifs which are otherwise foreign to that figure.

There are many problems presented by these twelve references which cannot be discussed here.[209] I have already pointed out the Evangelist's creativity, as well as his purpose, in linking an act of Moses together with an act done to the Son of Man (3:14). At the present juncture we may turn our attention (a) to the motifs given in 9:35 ff. and (b) to the way in which John speaks about the Son of Man's ascent to the Father. The two aspects of the Johannine Son of Man which will emerge as we do this betray John's hand quite as clearly as does the linking of the Son of Man with Moses.

(a) None of John's pictures of the Son of Man is more surprising than the one given in 9:35 ff. Nowhere else in gospel tradition does the Jesus who walks among men on the face of the earth require of someone the confession of himself as the Son of Man. In the famous Caesarea Philippi pericope this title is not even mentioned as a possible one for Jesus, and that is hardly surprising. One would scarcely think of confessing an earthbound figure as the heavenly Son of Man. There is, to be sure, a stratum in the synoptic tradition in which Jesus refers to himself in the midst of his earthly activity as the Son of Man, but that is quite another matter. H. E. Tödt is correct when he speaks of this synoptic phenomenon as a *prolepsis* which arose mainly because of the continuity between Jesus and the Son of Man expressed in the saying:

Everyone who acknowledges me before men, the Son of Man
· will also acknowledge before the angels of God. (Luke 12:8)[210]

John 9:35, on the other hand, can scarcely be spoken of as an instance of *prolepsis.* On the contrary, we must speak in this case of the *presence* of the Son of Man in the world. As Ernst Käsemann remarks, for John

[209]The literature on the Johannine Son of Man is extensive. See particularly S. S. Smalley, "The Johannine Son of Man Sayings," *NTS* 15 (1968/69), 278-301; R. G. Hamerton-Kelly, *Preexistence, Wisdom and the Son of Man* (1973); E. Ruckstuhl, "Die johanneische Menschensohnforschung 1957–1969," J. Pfammatter und F. Furger (eds.), *Theologische Berichte* I (1972), 171-284; W. A. Meeks, "The Man from Heaven"; Ruckstuhl, "Abstieg und Erhöhung des johanneischen Menschensohns," R. Pesch und R. Schnackenburg (eds.), *Jesus und der Menschensohn, für Anton Vögtle* (1975), pp. 314-41; J. Coppens, "Les logia johanniques du fils de l'homme," M. de Jonge (ed.), *L'Evangile de Jean,* pp. 311-15.
[210]Tödt, *The Son of Man,* p. 295.

Jesus is the Son of Man because in him the Son of God comes to man. It characterizes John's radical re-interpretation that he uses this title which designated the apocalpytic World Judge to refer to the earthly existence of Jesus.[211]

Nor did John arrive at this portrait of Jesus as the Son of Man present among men on earth by slightly modifying the proleptic use of the title in synoptic tradition.[212] He came to it for reasons which are closely bound up with the two-level drama, as 9:35 ff. clearly tells us. It is centrally as the Son of Man that Jesus appears on the contemporary level of the drama and thus makes known his presence. The traditional motif of the Son of Man as judge, so prominent in 5:27, is directly acted out in 9:35-41. In the midst of the church-synagogue tension of his own day John hears the Son of Man say:

> For judgment I came into this world, that those who do not see may see, and that those who see may become blind. (9:39)

It is precisely the contemporary level of the drama which makes clear that judgment by the Son of Man takes place essentially on earth and in the present, not in heaven and in the future. Indeed, in order to avoid misunderstanding, we should say that the judging and redeeming presence of the Son of Man is limited neither to a past epoch during which Jesus was in the world nor to a future point of cosmic upheaval. In John's own time and place Jesus somehow makes effective his presence as the Son of Man.

(b) The picture is, however, by no means consistent. We have seen that a number of John's references to the Son of Man speak of his ascension, his being lifted up, his being glorified (3:14; 6:62; 12:23, etc.). This motif may be indebted to speculation in which the figure of wisdom descends and ascends, as well as to the Christian tradition of the necessity of Jesus' death. As Barrett remarks, the Son of Man "returns where he was before (cf. 1:1) by mounting upon the cross."[213] It is also said that when the Son

---

[211]Käsemann, *Testament*, p. 13.
[212]Cf. R. Schnackenburg, "Der Menschensohn im Johannesevangelium," *NTS*, 11/2 (1965), pp. 123-37: "Der vierte Evangelist [ist] zu seinen Gegenwartsaussagen über den Menschensohn nicht über die synoptische Tradition gekommen . . . , sondern auf eigenen Wegen theologischen Weiterdenkens" (p. 131).
[213]Barrett, *St. John*, p. 250.

of Man is lifted up *from the earth,* he will draw all men to himself (12:32).[214] We have already noted that in John's affirmation of the Son of Man's ascension there is surely a polemical note vis à vis claims the synagogue is making for Moses. Wayne Meeks has cogently argued that John probably worded 3:13 as it stands in order categorically to exclude the rather exotic traditions about Moses' (and Elijah's) ascent.[215] Beyond clearly presenting such a polemic, however, 3:13 provides a somewhat confusing picture with respect to the locus of the Son of Man. Here, while conversing with Nicodemus, Jesus speaks as though he were already exalted to heaven:

> No one *has* ascended into heaven but he who descended from heaven, the Son of Man. (3:13)

An ancient scribe sensed the implication of the fact that the first verb is in the perfect tense when he added to this sentence the words, "who is in heaven." Even without his addition the verse is highly ambiguous. Jesus is portrayed conversing with Nicodemus on earth; yet he speaks at this point as though he had already ascended to heaven. In light of these references it is clear that John's Son of Man is not consistently located on earth.

This difficulty is considerably compounded when we recall the very promise of Jesus which initially helped us to discover the two-level drama:

> He who believes in me will also do the works that I do; and greater works than these will he do, because I go to the Father. (14:12)

When we first quoted this verse, we were intent on the literary and historical analysis of John 9. Now we must consider the highly paradoxical character of the verse when it is taken together with the two-level drama toward which it points. Jesus promises the Johannine church that his followers will continue to

---

[214]This note may be a re-interpretation of the apocalyptic hope of being gathered around the Son of Man in heaven as one sees it in I Enoch 62 quoted above.

[215]Meeks, *Prophet-King,* p. 301. Regarding the possible role of 3:13 as polemic against Elijah traditions see Martyn, "We Have Found Elijah," and cf. P. Borgen, "Some Jewish Exegetical Traditions as Background for Son of Man Sayings in John's Gospel (Jn 3, 13-14 and context)," M. de Jonge (ed.), *L'Evangile de Jean,* pp. 243-58.

do his works, and that is exactly what we found to be characteristic of the two-level drama. But whereas in that drama his followers continue to do his works because he makes known his *presence* in the everyday fabric of life, he clearly says in the promise that all of this will take place because he is *going to the Father.*[216]

This paradox presents to us the same problem posed by the apparent inconsistency with regard to the present locale of the Son of Man. Is Jesus as the Son of Man now with the Father or with his followers on earth? If the two-level drama takes place "because I go to the Father," is the risen Lord now in heaven or making his presence known in the everyday life of John's community? In order to attack this problem in a way which follows the grain of John's thought we must recognize that the paradoxical promise of 14:12 occurs immediately prior to the first of five passages in which Jesus promises the coming of the Paraclete.

4. The Paraclete, the Son of Man, and the Two-Level Drama

Whatever the ultimate origin of the figure called the Paraclete, the main lines of the interpretation laid on him by John are clear

---

[216]We may recall our discussion (pp. 28 ff.) of the similar tension posed in 9:4 f. (a) The expression "*We* must work the works of him who sent *me*" points, I said, to a two-level drama in which Jesus' works are continued as he effects his presence in and through the Christian witness. (b) On the other hand, the words which follow speak of a time when no one can work. Furthermore, Jesus explicitly says, "While I am in the world, I am the light of the world." The tension between these two motifs is to be taken seriously. It points to what Bultmann has correctly termed the Johannine "too late" (*Johannes,* pp. 231 ff.). Jesus' departure from the world signifies for those who do not believe a point after which it is "too late." This is clear on the *einmalig* level of the drama: The people with whom Jesus comes into contact have only "the day" as their opportunity. Jesus dies, not as a result of their sovereign will; his departure to the Father is, rather, his own deed. For the world this departure of Jesus signifies the judgment (8:28; 16:8-11; 8:21-24) in this way: when he is gone, there will be no more revelation for them. But now we must also inquire into the meaning which this "too late" has on the contemporary level. Does it signify that Jesus' works have come to an end, as Bernard says (*St. John,* Vol. II, p. 326)? I think not. It does mean that in the moment of unfaith, it is already "too late." Just as in the time of Jesus' earthly life, so also now his words spoken through the Christian witness, his deeds performed in the Christian preacher, are not objects toward which one may take a stand today or tomorrow. They are, rather, the words and deeds of the sovereign Son of Man who judges in the moment itself. There is a "too late," therefore, on both the *einmalig* and the contemporary levels of the drama, but the awesome meaning which this "too late" has for John would be wholly lost if we compelled him to speak of a time in which Jesus *was* the Light of the World, a time in which he *was* the Bread of Life, a time in which he *was* the Son of Man.

enough.[217] These lines of interpretation may be readily grasped if we first summarize the characteristics of the Johannine Paraclete and then consider the manner in which John allows Jesus to introduce his promises about the Paraclete.

14:15-17

1. Jesus will intercede with the Father in behalf of the disciples, and the Father will give them *another* Paraclete.
2. This other Paraclete will be with the disciples forever, in apparent contrast to Jesus who is now taking leave of them.
3. The other Paraclete is the Spirit of Truth.
4. He is invisible to the world; it neither sees nor knows him.
5. But the disciples know him, for he abides with them and will be in them (cf. 20:22).

14:25-26

6. The Paraclete is the Holy Spirit.
7. He will teach the believers all things, and
8. he will bring to their remembrance all that Jesus has said to them.

[217]See the excellent study by Otto Betz, *Der Paraklet, Fürsprecher im häretischen Spätjudentum, im Johannes-evangelium und in neu-gefundenen gnostischen Schriften* (1963), where all of the literature to its date is cited. Worthy of special mention are G. Bornkamm, "Der Paraklet im Johannesevangelium," pp. 12-35 in *Festschrift Rudolf Bultmann* (1949), and S. Schulz, *Menschensohn-Christologie*. Bornkamm's thesis, accepted by Schulz, that the essential features of the Paraclete are derived from Jewish expectations of the Son of Man, is not quite so far wide of the mark as Betz thinks. The thesis is surely incorrect as it stands, but it points to the fact that in one important respect the *Johannine* Paraclete looks very much like the *Johannine* Son of Man: both judge the world. Regarding the ultimate origin of the Paraclete figure, Betz's parallels drawn from the literature of Qumran are impressive; but see the criticisms of Schnackenburg, *St. John*, p. 134, and of Raymond Brown, "The Paraclete in the Fourth Gsopel," *NTS* 13/2 (1967), 113-32, especially pp. 125 f. See further G. Johnston, *The Spirit-Paraclete in the Gospel of John* (1970); A. R. C. Leaney, "The Johannine Paraclete and the Qumran Scrolls," J. H. Charlesworth (ed.), *John and Qumran* (1972), pp. 38-61; U. B. Müller, "Die Parakletenvorstellung im Johannesevangelium," *ZThK* 71 (1974), 31-77; I. de la Potterie, "Parole et esprit dans S. Jean," de Jonge (ed.), *L'Evangile de Jean*, pp. 177-210. The article by Müller is especially percipient and constitutes a genuine step forward, even if all aspects of the argument are not fully convincing.

15:26-27

    9. The Paraclete will bear witness to Jesus.

16:5-11

    10. When the Paraclete comes, he will act as prosecuting attorney and judge with regard to the world; he will convict the world.

16:12-15

    11. The Paraclete will not speak on his own authority; he will glorify Jesus, taking that which is Jesus' and declaring it to the believers.

    12. He will declare to the believers the things that are to come.

From this sketch alone it is clear that the Paraclete looks very much like Jesus. He is the *other* Paraclete, Jesus being the first Paraclete. He has no independent "personality." He has no independent function. His sole *raison d'être* is

    to bring to the disciples' remembrance all that Jesus said,
    to bear witness to Jesus,
    to glorify Jesus,
    to continue Jesus' "suit with the world."

That the Paraclete continues Jesus' "suit with the world" suggests that his function is closely related to Jesus' office as the Son of Man. We have already seen that judgment at the hands of the Son of Man is for the Fourth Evangelist emphatically an event of the present. Now we see how the Son of Man's presence is effected. By continuing Jesus' "suit with the world" the Paraclete makes effective Jesus' presence as the awesome Son of Man. Here we may see the reason for John's inconsistency regarding the locale of that awesome figure. The Son of Man ascends to heaven on the cross, but in some sense he returns to earth in the person of the Paraclete and can therefore enter into conversation with "Nicodemus" as he who *has ascended* to heaven (3:13). The Paraclete makes Jesus present on earth as the Son of Man who binds together heaven and earth (1:51). Therefore the Son of Man cannot be located exclusively either in heaven or on earth.

    The Paraclete plays a similar role with regard to the two-level drama. If we ask why the second Paraclete should look so much like the first, the answer is immediately at hand: the second

Paraclete looks like the first for the sake of the two-level drama. Here the contexts in which John allows Jesus to make his promises about the Paraclete are extremely important. One of the "red lines" which runs through the whole complex of the Farewell Discourses is, of course, the problem which is posed by Jesus' departure. John 13 opens with the awesome note that Jesus' hour has come to depart out of this world to the Father (v. 1). The reader has been told many times that the world is, so to speak, foreign territory to the Revealer.[218] He was the mediator of creation, but he is also "from above," and that statement about his origin also says something about his destiny. Now it is time for him to return from the world to the Father with whom he dwelt before the world was made (17:5). This line of thought is quite central to John's theology. On the cross Jesus really ascends to the Father. In anticipation of that real departure he says in his great prayer to the Father:

> And now I am no longer in the world, but they are in the world. . . . While I was with them, I kept them in thy name. (17:11 f.)

This turn of events is bound to put fear into the hearts of Jesus' disciples. They are left behind in "enemy territory" without their leader. From their point of view the Lord is departing in midstream, so to speak. To be sure, he utters from the cross the victorious cry "It is finished." That tells us very forcefully that there is no *second* drama which will be the sequel to the drama of God's sending his Son (contrast Luke-Acts). But in itself that magnificent cry does not solve the problem of the separation caused by Jesus' departure, and this problem is one of the main subjects of the Farewell Discourses. Whereas the Redeemer is now returning to heaven, his disciples must remain in the world.

At this point a number of options were open to the theologian in John's place. Let me mention two of them, since they play a role in the Farewell Discourses.[219] The author of I Enoch 39

---

[218]The Revealer is thus the Stranger to the world, as E. Käsemann, *Testament,* p. 22, and particularly W. A. Meeks, "Man from Heaven," *passim,* have noted.

[219]A third possibility must also be mentioned, even though we cannot pause here to develop it: A "realistic" or "Ignatian" understanding of the Eucharist would serve to bridge the chasm between the departed Lord and his followers. It is this problem of separation which is the greater scandal mentioned in 6:62. And the greater scandal is met *to an extent* by the lesser scandal (vs. 54). But 6:63 shows clearly that John does not elect to solve the problem posed in the Farewell Discourses by a realistic understanding of the Eucharist. Against G. Bornkamm,

speaks of the dwelling places of the holy ones, the resting places of the righteous in heaven (vs. 4). Similarly in II Enoch we hear that God has prepared many mansions in heaven, good for the good and bad for the bad (61:2). A theologian faced with the problem posed by the Redeemer's departure could have the Redeemer speak comfortingly about heavenly resting places.

Alternatively he could allow the Redeemer to talk of a mystical union between himself and his own, spanning the distance between them by taking the believer out of the world, at least in mystic trances. The religious literature of the Hellenistic age abounds with motifs easily employed in order to make this point.

John allows the departing Lord to elect both of these options; yet he has the Lord do so in a sovereign manner. Jesus tells his sorrowing disciples not to be troubled, assuring them that there are many rooms in his Father's house. He then changes the terms of the picture radically by saying that he will come again and take them not to these rooms but to himself. Furthermore:

> If a man loves me, he will keep my word, and my Father will love him, and we will come to him and make our home with him (14:23; the term rendered "home" is μονη, the same term rendered "rooms" in 14:2).

Thus, the problem of separation is ultimately to be met with the preparation not of rooms, but of a room, and that room is not in heaven, but on earth. The disciple can overcome his fear and make his way in the period after Jesus' departure not by recalling that at the close of his own lifetime there will be a room for him in heaven, but rather by knowing that in the present time both the Father and the Son come and make their home with him.

Similarly, while Jesus speaks of a remarkable union between himself and his followers, using the ancient imagery of the vine with its branches, the resulting picture is neither mystical nor otherworldly.

"Die eucharistische Rede im Johannesevangelium," *ZNW,* 47 (1956), pp. 161-169, E. Schweizer, "Das johanneische Zeugnis vom Herrenmahl," *EvTh,* 12 (1952/3), pp. 358-361 and P. Borgen, *Bread from Heaven,* accept 6:51*b*-59 as Johannine. Borgen's argument is particularly impressive. See also C. K. Barrett, "Das Fleisch des Menschensohns (Joh 6.53)," R. Pesch und R. Schnackenburg (eds.), *Jesus und der Menschensohn* (1975), pp. 342-54.

I do not pray that thou shouldst take them out of the world, but that thou shouldst keep them from the evil one. (17:15)

For immediately following his words about the vine, the Risen Lord makes clear that the union about which he has spoken is played out in the earthy drama of everyday life.

If the world hates you, know that it hated me before it hated you. . . . If they persecuted me, they will persecute you. . . . They will put you out of the synagogues; indeed the hour is coming when whoever kills you (because you are a beguiler) will think he is offering service to God. (15:18, 20; 16:2)

Thus, John has Jesus modify the traditional hope for rooms in heaven by speaking about a home on earth. This modification brings with it the promise of Jesus' own return to his disciples. John also allows Jesus to employ the imagery of mystic union, but that union takes on its notes of world-foreignness precisely in the *two*-level drama which involves such earthy things as the painful amputation from the synagogue and facing trial on the charge of being a beguiler.

If we now return to the Paraclete passages, reading them in the context thus outlined, we see that of all the functions of the Paraclete, none is more central than his continuing the work of Jesus. The paradox presented by Jesus' promise that his work on earth will be continued because he is going to the Father is "solved" by his return in the person of the Paraclete. *It is, therefore, precisely the Paraclete who creates the two-level drama.* One cannot fail to be impressed by the boldness with which John reinterprets the traditional motif of the coming of the Spirit. That is especially true when we recognize that in order for the Paraclete to create the two-level drama, he must look not only like Jesus, but also like the Christian witness who is Jesus' "double" in that drama:

Jesus	The Other Paraclete	The Christian Witness
a. Origin		
I came from the Father (16:27 and many others), I came not of	The Paraclete who proceeds from the Father (15:26); the Paraclete	As thou didst send me into the world, so I have sent them into the

148

Jesus	The Other Paraclete	The Christian Witness
my own accord, but he sent me. (8:42, etc.)	whom the Father will send. (14:26)	world. (17:18)

b. Coming

I will come to you. (14:18, 28)	When the Paraclete comes. (15:26, etc.)	[The motif is, of course, absent.]

c. Relationship to the world
1. The world does not know:

You know neither me nor my Father. (8:19, cf. 17: 25)	Whom the world cannot receive because it neither sees him nor knows him. (14:17)	[The reason why the world does not know us is that it did not know him. (1 John 3:1)]

2. The world hates:

Know that the world hated me before it hated you. (15:18)	The Paraclete . . . whom the world cannot receive. (14:17)	If the world hates you . . . (15:18)

3. The world is judged:

And this is judgment, that the light has come into the world, and men loved darkness rather than light. (3:19) He who does not believe is condemned already. (3:18)	And when he comes, he will convince the world of sin and of righteousness and of judgment. . . . (16:8 ff.)	Jesus [in the person of the Christian witness] said, "For judgment I came into the world, that those who do not see may see, and that those who see may become blind." (9:39)

d. Teaching under authority

My teaching is not mine (7:16). I have not spoken on my own authority (12:49; cf. 14:24).	He will not speak on his own authority. (16:13)	As thou didst send me into the world, so I have sent them into the world. (17:18)

e. Bearing witness . . .

I bear witness to myself. (8:14)	He will bear witness to me. (15:26)	And you also are witnesses. (15:27)

Truly, truly I say to you, *we* speak of what we know, and bear witness to what we have seen; but you do not receive our testimony. (3:11)

f. . . . in such a way as to extend Jesus' work into the present.

These things I have spoken to you, while I am still with you. (14:25)	But the Paraclete . . . will teach you all things, and bring to your remembrance all that I have said to you. (14:26) He will declare to you the things that are to come. He will glorify me, for he will take what is mine and declare it to you. (16:13 f.)	Truly, truly I say to you, he who believes in me will also do the works that I do; and greater works than these will he do, because I go to the Father. (14:12)

We must work the works of him who sent *me* while it is day. (9:4)

149

The coming of the Paraclete is the return of Jesus to his own. They are now in him and he in them (14:20). But it is a dramatic union played out in the two-level drama in a way which creates an epistemological crisis. The world sees, of course, only one level of the drama. It sees the *einmalig* tradition about Jesus of Nazareth, a figure of the past (14:19), whose identity may be debated in a midrashic manner. Or it sees the contemporary Christian, without perceiving the Paraclete who makes Jesus present in the Christian's deeds and words (14:17). For John, on the other hand, the drama is real precisely because it is played simultaneously on the two levels. We may recall the initial climax which John creates in the prologue to his Gospel:

And the word became flesh and dwelt among us, full of grace and truth; we beheld his glory, glory as of the only Son of the Father. (1:14)[220]

And we may compare with it two of the verses from the Farewell Discourses which have already claimed our attention. Just as the Word did not remain in heaven, but rather came and dwelt among us,[221] so the Risen Lord does not remain in heaven, but rather comes to dwell with his own.

If a man loves me, he will keep my word, and my Father will love him, and we will come and make our home with him. (14:23)

Furthermore, John can say in his prologue "we beheld his glory" not only because the Christian church possesses tradition about Jesus' *einmalig* revelation of the Father, but also because the Paraclete is even now showing Jesus in his glory.

He will glorify me, for he will take what is mine and declare it to you. (16:14)

The two-level drama makes clear that the Word's dwelling among us and our beholding his glory are not events which transpired only in the past. They do not constitute an ideal period

[220]E. Käsemann has convincingly shown that this verse is John's initial comment on the Logos Hymn which he employed to introduce his gospel, "The Structure and Purpose of the Prologue to John's Gospel," pp. 138-67 in *New Testament Questions of Today* (1969).

[221]E. Haenchen has developed this motif in a very helpful way, "Probleme des johanneischen Prologs," *ZThK*, 60/3 (1963), pp. 305-34.

when the kingdom of God was on earth, a period to which one looks back with the knowledge that it has now drawn to a close with Jesus' ascension to heaven as the Son of Man. These events to which John bears witness transpire on both the *einmalig* and the contemporary levels of the drama, or they do not transpire at all. In John's view, their transpiring on both levels of the drama is, to a large extent, the good news itself.

Excursuses

Excursus A

Luke 13:10-17

There are in the Synoptic Gospels five accounts of three stories in which Jesus heals on the sabbath: Mark 3:1-5 (parallels Matt. 12:9-13 and Luke 6:6-10), Luke 14:1-6, and Luke 13:10-17. The first of these, Mark 3:1-5, may have served as the pattern for the others. In any event, four of the five accounts show a common structure.

1. It is the sabbath; three of the four accounts place the events in a synagogue.
2. A sick person is present; Jesus' critics watch to see if he will heal the person, thus breaking the sabbath.
3. Jesus proposes to heal the sick person in spite of the sabbath law against work; he directs sharp remarks to his critics.
4. His remarks silence the critics, or at least meet no opposition; in one of the stories (Luke 14:1-6) this element is given twice (v. 3-4a and v. 5-6).
5. Jesus heals the sick person.

The fidelity of the four accounts to this structure (Bultmann calls them apophthegms, *History, ad. loc.*) serves to accent the divergence of the story in Luke 13. There the form is as follows:

1. It is the sabbath; Jesus teaches in a synagogue.
2. A sick person is present.
3. Jesus heals the person.
4. The ruler of the synagogue (Rosh ha-Keneset) becomes angry and exhorts the congregation not to allow healings on the sabbath.
5. Jesus enters into dialogue with the ruler of the synagogue and other critics, presumably the elders of the synagogue.
6. As a result, the critics are shamed; all the people rejoice at the glorious things done by Jesus.

153

In this case someone has apparently altered the course of events. The critical remarks of Jesus, the third element in the earlier pattern, have undergone two changes: (a) They have been expanded into a *dialogue* between Jesus and the synagogue ruler, so that the opposition is no longer silent, and (b) this dialogue now comes *after* rather than before the miracle, even at the price of separating verse 17*b* (the crowd's rejoicing) from the deed to which it refers.

It is important to ask why these changes were made and whether they reflect a specific situation which we may at least partially reconstruct. I do not propose to deal with these questions in detail just here, but I think enough has been said to suggest that the creation of a dialogue in place of Jesus' unanswered remarks may reflect later church-synagogue conversations. Luke—not to mention earlier traditioners—certainly knew something about the order of synagogue worship (Luke 4) and may have heard critical remarks from a synagogue ruler somewhat like those given in 13:14. Furthermore, the placing of the dialogue after the miracle serves to accent that dialogue rather than the cure. This change may reflect the opinion of a Christian editor that the church-synagogue conversation is what needs illumination from such a pericope.

Thus, Luke 13:10-17 may reflect, in part, critical conversation between synagogue and church. However that may be, the instructive thing for us is the wide divergence between even this piece and the drama which lies before us in John 9. For in the latter passage one sees the following unique elements:

1. There is a *succession* of *scenes,* each of which is realistically conceived, with its own climax, but also executed in a way which serves the drama as a whole. Luke 13:10-17 presents *one scene.*
2. Interest in the healed person, far from ceasing after the cure, intensifies, and he is made a major actor in four of the following six scenes. Luke 13:10-17, on the other hand, remains essentially in the miracle-story form by allowing the healed person to fall from sight once the cure is effected.
3. It is true that Luke 13:14 introduces a character not explicitly mentioned earlier, the synagogue ruler. His

presence is presumed, however, from the beginning, since the scene is set as sabbath worship in a synagogue. The drama in John 9, on the other hand, is unfolded partly by introducing several new characters in new locales as events proceed and as one scene is replaced by another.

Thus, the net effect drawn from this comparison of sabbath healings is to accent once again the elements which are peculiar to the Johannine account and which scarcely came "out of the air."

Excursus B

The Synagogue Ban

Modern investigation of the Jewish ban apparently began with Elias Levita (died 1549), who found in the rabbinic literature references to three levels of the ban: נדוי, חרם, and שמתא. Buxtorf and Schürer reduced the number to two, showing that נדוי and שמתא are alternate names for temporary exclusion from the community, while חרם refers to a permanent ban: Schürer, *Jewish People,* Division II, Vol. II, pp. 60 ff. Schürer speculated that in Jesus' time both types of ban were employed, the heavier type being accompanied by the pronouncement of αναωεμα (the Pauline passages are discussed by Schürer on p. 61). Luke 6:22, John 9:22; 12:42, and 16:2 Schürer considered to be references to the Jewish ban, though they give no direct hint as to the type referred to.

Johannine interpreters have often followed this lead, as the entry in Bauer's lexicon and Bauer's remarks in his own commentary suggest (*Johannes,* p. 131). At the appropriate places in their commentaries Hoskyns, Büchsel, Howard, Lightfoot, Bernard, Schlatter, and Bultmann all identify the Johannine references with the Jewish ban. As one would expect, Schlatter's comment is the most specific of the group. From *Sifre Numbers* 105 he quoted a reference to disciplinary measures accorded Akabiya:

עקביה נתנדה

In his customary way Schlatter gave a Greek translation:

ακαβια αποσυναγωγος εγενετο,

thus suggesting that αποσυναγωγος γενεσθαι is the equivalent of נתנדה (the Nithpael of נדה), the imposition of the lighter form of ban.

Schlatter's argument is impressive, as usual, but several factors militate against it. The reference to Akabiya's treatment is a convenient place to begin, for particularly the fuller account in *Mishna Eduyoth* 5, 6 does indeed invite comparison of the rabbinic נדוי with the Johannine αποσυναγωγος γενεσθαι.

Excursus B

According to *Eduyoth* 5, 6 Akabiya (pre-Tannaitic, ca. C.E. 50 or 60) expressed four halakic opinions at variance with those of the sages. Offered the second position in the Sanhedrin if he withdrew these opinions, Akabiya refused. Subsequently he was laid under a ban (נדה). Indeed, he died "while he was yet under the ban, and the court stoned his coffin."

The words quoted give us two important data. (1) That Akabiya is said to have died while yet under the ban tells us that the *niddui* was intended to be temporary. Its purpose was not permanently to separate someone from the community. Quite the contrary. The Sanhedrin layed Akabiya under the ban in the hope of his recanting specific halakic opinions. (2) The court's act of stoning his coffin shows that Akabiya, though under the ban, remained subject to Jewish authority. The first of these points is effectively stated by Billerbeck at the conclusion of his examination of the rabbinic evidence; I have quoted his words above (p. 44). To sharpen the issue with respect to the second point, we may say that *within* the Jewish community or synagogue one member may be placed under the *niddui*. If, then, we follow Schlatter's lead in seeking a Greek translation for נתנדה, we must render it in a way which makes plain that the banned person remains essentially εν τη συναγωγη and is therefore not απο συναγωγης.

But if the Johannine expression is not illuminated by the *niddui*, perhaps it corresponds to the more severe *cherem*. Here we encounter the important work of Claus-Hunno Hunzinger, *Die jüdische Bannpraxis im neutestamentlichen Zeitalter*, Dissertation, Göttingen, 1954 (see also *ThLZ* 80 [1955], 114 f.), who argues conclusively that a careful dating of the rabbinic materials shows no reference to *cherem* with the meaning "ban" or "excommunicate" prior to the third century C.E. Thus, in the first and second centuries only the *niddui* can come into consideration. In light of what I have said above about Akabiya, one is not surprised to find Hunzinger arguing that the *niddui* was used only to protect halakic tradition and that it was usually employed, therefore, only against scholars.

The net result, of course, is that while the Jewish ban practice may be somehow related to the Johannine expression, it can scarcely provide the main clue for the historical identification of that expression.

Excursus C

πλαναν and יסת, סות

Dr. Ed P. Sanders kindly called to my attention the possibility of a second line of argument supporting the thesis that behind John's use of the verb πλαναν in 7:47 stands the technical, rabbinic use of the verb יסת, סות. It seems to me to be just that, a supporting line of argument which is helpful when the probability of the thesis has been accepted on other grounds.

As one ponders the way in which the authorities angrily reproach their police for failing to apprehend Jesus, one sees that they pose two alternatives: a man who listens to Jesus (7:46) may *be led astray* (πεπλανησθαι), or he may withhold himself from *believing in Jesus* (μη πιστευσαι εις αυτον). These alternatives might be expressed in Greek as follows:

a. πεπλανησθε πιστευσαι εις αυτον
   You are led astray to believe in him.
b. οι φαρισαιοι ουκ επιστευσαν εις αυτον
   The Pharisees (not having been led astray) did not believe in him.

While John does not actually provide the verb πλαναν with the epexegetical infinitive πιστευσαι, the immediate context strongly suggests this as a construction appropriate to his meaning. The possibility which the authorities consider in 7:47, however distantly, is not merely that their police have been misled. It is that the police have been led astray so as to believe in *Jesus.*

It is surprising to find that the verb πλαναν is used in precisely this way relatively infrequently. It generally means "to cause to wander," "deceive" (active), "wander," "stray," "be misled" (passive), rather than "to lead astray into the doing of something which constitutes false practice." Liddell-Scott lists no instance in which there is a clear parallel to the meaning required of the

Excursus C

verb in John 7:47, and though I chanced across one in Epictetus (3, 22, 23: πλαναν with epexegetical infinitive), I have found none among the references (classical and Hellenistic) given by H. Braun in his article on πλαναν in *ThWNT*. There is a single parallel in the New Testament, and it is quite revealing.

> But I have this against you, that you tolerate the woman Jezebel, who calls herself a prophetess and is teaching and beguiling my servants to practice immorality and to eat food sacrificed to idols. (Rev. 2:20)

Here is a sentence which presents two syntactical problems recognized by commentators: (1) the case of the participle η λεγουσα with which one may compare LXX at Zeph. 1:12, and (2) the inconsistency created by allowing finite verbs to stand in parallel with this participle: η λεγουσα . . . διδασκει και πλανα . . . . While I should not call it a problem in the strict sense, a third syntactical phenomenon calls for comment, although it has received none from the interpreters I have consulted: the verb πλαναν is provided with epexegetical infinitives. The two problems with which interpreters *have* concerned themselves clearly stand in the Greek text because of the influence of Hebrew syntax. Should we say the same of the construction involving the verb πλαναν?

A review of certain data in LXX and in rabbinic literature leads to an affirmative answer. Let me summarize:

1. סות, יסת is used in the Old Testament and in rabbinic literature, sometimes with the infinitive construct, sometimes only with a clearly implied verbal supplement, to mean "lead astray to do something." See, for example, Judges 1:14; 1 Chronicles 21:1; 2 Chronicles 18:2; 32:11; *Sanhedrin* 61a (עבד); and compare *Sifre Deuteronomy* 89. When it is so used in the Old Testament, it is often rendered by either πειθω or απαταω plus infinitive.

2. The Hiphil of תעה is used in the Old Testament, sometimes with the infinitive construct, sometimes only with a clearly implied verbal supplement, to mean essentially the same thing. See, for example, 4 Kings 21:9; 2 Chronicles 33:9; and compare *Sanhedrin* 55a, where the context makes clear that the leading astray is a seduction to false worship. When

the verb is so used in the Old Testament, it is rendered by πλαναω plus infinitive.

Thus, it is apparently natural in religious texts composed in Hebrew and Aramaic to specify a verb meaning "mislead" or something similar by providing an epexegetical infinitive or by clearly implying a verbal supplement. It is apparently for this reason that the verb πλαναν is given an epexegetical infinitive in LXX.

When we now return to Revelation 2:20 and to John 7:47, the first of which presents us with πλαναν plus epexegetical infinitive and the second of which clearly implies the sense of that construction, we are impressed with the possibility that both passages reflect the use of סות, יסת or תעה. If this possibility should seem to be probability, as I am inclined to say it does because of the other Hebraisms in Revelation 2:20, then for our present purposes John 7:47 may be somewhat undertranslated when rendered

"Don't tell us you have been fooled too!" The Pharisees retorted. (Brown, *John*, p. 319)

It would perhaps be better to render it, as does *NEB*,

The Pharisees retorted, "Have you too been misled?"

Indeed a full and interpretative paraphrase, composed with an eye to 5:18 as well as to the immediate context, would be

"Have you too been led astray to believe in him as a second god?" replied the Pharisees.

That is to say, the Pharisees (the Gerousia of John's city) express concern about the favorable attitude which their police take toward Jesus because, even without having held a formal trial, they have reached the conclusion that Jesus (a Jewish-Christian missioner in John's city) is a *Mesith*. It is against the reaching of this conclusion without a formal trial, not against the Pharisees' rough handling of their police, that Nicodemus objects in 7:51.

John 7:45-52 and Acts 5

In our analysis of John 7:45-52 (chap. 4), we will suggest that for the characters there portrayed John drew most of his inspiration from the actual experiences of his church. "The Pharisees" act like the Jamnia Loyalists who dominate the Gerousia of John's city. "The police" function somewhat as *Chazzanim* known to John. And "the rulers," especially represented by Nicodemus, stand for the secretly believing faction in the Gerousia. All of this does not mean, however, that the *literary problems* posed by these verses have been solved. That is to say, John may have drawn not only on the experience of his church, but also on Christian tradition. One factor in particular points toward that conclusion: the role played by Nicodemus.

Even a casual reading suffices to show how closely the role of Nicodemus corresponds to the one played by Gamaliel in Acts 5. And a careful comparison reveals a still more remarkable degree of correspondence:

1. Nicodemus and Gamaliel

John 3	Acts 5
νικοδημος ονομα αυτω	ονοματι γαμαλιηλ
αρχων των ιουδαιων	τις εν τω συνεδριω
εκ των φαρισαιων	φαρισαιος
ο διδασκαλος του ισραηλ	νομοδιδασκαλος τιμιος παντι τω λαω

It is natural enough that in introducing the men, the authors state their names. Beyond this, both are members of the Sanhedrin, both are of the Pharisaic party, and each is explicitly said to be a "teacher" (a rabbi). Thus, even apart from their acts, they are introduced in remarkably similar terms.

History and Theology in the Fourth Gospel

2. The dramatis personae

John 7	Acts 5
The Sanhedrin	The Sanhedrin
οι αρχιερεις και οι φαρισαιοι	ο αρχιερευς και παντες οι συν αυτω
	το συνεδριον
	πασα η γερουσια των υιων ισραηλ
The Temple police	The Temple police
υπηρεται	υπηρεται
	(overseen by the στρατηγος του ιερου)
Jesus	The apostles
ο ιησους	οι αποστολοι
The defender	The defender
νικοδημος	γαμαλιηλ

e. *Common motifs in the dramas*
  a. Teaching in the Temple:
    εν τω ιερω διδασκων (John 7:28; cf. 7:14)
    εισηλθον . . . εις το ιερον και εδιδασκον (Acts 5:21; cf. 5:12, 25) (Cf. also Acts 5:12 and John 10:22 regarding Solomon's portico in the Temple.)
  b. Sanhedrin aroused to terminate the teaching by an arrest:
    απεστειλαν οι αρχιερεις και οι φαρισαιοι υπηρετας ινα πιασωσιν αυτον (John 7:32)
    ο αρχιερευς και παντες οι συν αυτω . . . επλησθησαν ζηλου και επεβαλον τας χειρας επι τους αποστολους και εθεντο αυτους εν τηρησει δημοσια (Acts 5:17 f.)
  c. Temple police return to Sanhedrin empty-handed:
    John 7:45 // Acts 5:22
  d. A member of the Sanhedrin formulates a quasi-defense (climax):
    John 7:50 f. // Acts 5:34 ff.

There are, of course, a number of important differences between the stories, but the dramatis personae, the essential development of the drama, and particularly the role of the defender are all handled with a remarkable degree of similarity. It is, indeed, no accident that the author of *The Acts of Pilate* (an

162

early form of which may have been known to Justin, i.e., mid-second century: *RGG*³) allowed the figures of Nicodemus and Gamaliel to coalesce (5, 1). No doubt he knew both the Fourth Gospel and Acts; his superimposing the figure of Nicodemus on that of Gamaliel is nevertheless significant. Indeed, in light of the extensive correspondence shown above, one is tempted to suggest that there stands in the background a common tradition which has been creatively employed both by John and by Luke. And if that should be the case, it is clear that the traditional story would have had to do with the trial not of Jesus, but of a Christian before a Jewish court. If the traditional form of the story is fairly well preserved in Acts (4 and 5), then it probably concerned Christians on trial for an offense other than "leading the people astray." That element of the Jewish attack on the nascent church would then be either unknown to Luke or considered by him to be unimportant. In any event, the major suggestion brings us back to the thesis of our argument in chapter 3: In composing John 7, the Evangelist allowed a certain coalescence of the figures of Jesus and of Christians in his own community (and elsewhere?) whom the Gerousia wished to arrest and subject to a trial. And *in John's city,* the charge on the basis of which the Gerousia proceeded, at least in some cases, was that of "leading the people astray." [Further evidence and additional arguments are given in the second chapter of my book *The Gospel of John in Christian History* (1979).]

Excursus E

Bibliography Pertinent
to the Hypothesis
of a Signs Source

The hypothesis that in writing his Gospel John drew on written sources otherwise unknown to us is a relative late-comer to the scholarly scene. Two other views dominated that scene for a very long time, and they rendered wholly unnecessary the hypothesis of an unknown source.

For the bulk of Christian history the Gospel was thought to have been written by an eyewitness who would obviously have had little or no need to draw on written sources of any kind. Early in the present century the problems attendant to this view—problems sensed by some scholars long before—began to make themselves felt more and more widely. Today the vast majority of interpreters have concluded that the Gospel as we have it was not authored by an eyewitness.

When the eyewitness theory first began to be abandoned, it was quite naturally replaced for the most part by the theory that John drew on one or more of the Synoptics. Over a period of some duration scholars engaged in lively debates about the precise nature of the Evangelist's attitude toward his synoptic sources, but debates of this sort simply underlined the assumption that he did in fact know and use at least one of them.

For a great many interpreters the scene was radically altered in the years following 1938, for in that year P. Gardner-Smith published an extraordinarily succinct and tightly constructed argument for John's independence of the Synoptics: *Saint John and the Synoptic Gospels* (Cambridge, 1938). So influential was Gardner-Smith's work that by the end of the Second World War his followers came to represent the prevailing position. Weighty voices continued to be raised in favor of the theory of

164

dependence, notably those of C. K. Barrett, R. H. Lightfoot, and W. G. Kümmel; but from most quarters one heard that the tide had been turned by the argument of Gardner-Smith.

It was quite naturally in the context dominated by the view of John's independence from the Synoptics that theories of his dependence on otherwise unknown sources came into their own. Chief among these was the rather complex hypothesis of Rudolf Bultmann which is thoroughly displayed by D. Moody Smith, Jr. in *The Composition and Order of the Fourth Gospel:* Bultmann's Literary Theory (1965). Of Bultmann's hypothesis only the theory of a Signs Source survived the ensuing criticism, and it itself has been and is doubted or denied by some interpreters today. More of that shortly. On the whole the theory of a Signs Source has fared rather well, and a number of interpreters have given further refinements and modifications to it.

The following bibliography is designed to be of assistance to readers who wish to see how the hypothesis of a Signs Source has been developed and criticized since the labors of Bultmann. Those interested in the lines of research prior to Bultmann will find them admirably covered in the first chapter of the book by Robert T. Fortna, *The Gospel of Signs:* A Reconstruction of the Narrative Source Underlying the Fourth Gospel (1970). And for even greater detail one may consult the first chapter of Fortna's dissertation (Union Theological Seminary, 1965) and the fourth chapter of H. M. Teeple, *The Literary Origin of the Gospel of John* (1974).

I have indicated above that while the theory of a Signs Source was the sole survivor from Bultmann's complex hypothesis, it itself has been doubted or denied by a number of scholars. These interpreters fall into two major groups. One group holds that John drew neither on the Synoptics nor on a narrative source otherwise unknown to us, but rather on homilies and traditional fragments of various sorts. Some scholars who fall for the most part in this group also hold that the Gospel went through several editions, either in the Evangelist's own hands or in those of his followers, none of these editions usually being thought of as a pre-Johannine source in the proper sense. Taking into account the important differences among them, one may consult particularly the works below by Brown, Cullmann, Lindars, and Wilkens. The other group is engaged in renewed and vigorous

efforts at showing the Evangelist to have been dependent on one
or more of the Synoptics. Again, taking differences into account,
one may consult particularly the works below by Barrett,
Neirynck, and Sabbe. Boismard fits neatly into neither of these
groups. He holds that there were three distinct editions of the
fully Johannine Gospel, the second and third of these showing
dependence on the Synoptics. He also believes, however, that
the first edition, being independent of the Synoptics, drew
heavily on a gospel which he calls "Document C"; and one can
notice that this source is in some regards comparable to Fortna's
Signs Gospel.

When one reads these recent labors together with the earlier
ones by Barrett, Lightfoot, Kümmel *et al.,* one realizes that the
debates between the supporters and the opponents of the Signs
Source theory are likely to continue for quite some time. It seems
fair to say that on the whole the research done by supporters and
opponents alike has been illuminating to the interpretative task.
And while it would be highly presumptuous to predict the
outcome of the debates, I must say that the Signs Source theory
itself seems to me to enjoy a considerable degree of probability,
especially as it has been developed in the extraordinarily careful
analysis of Robert T. Fortna.

Bailey, J. A., *The Traditions Common to the Gospels of Luke and John* (Leiden, 1963).
Bammel, E., "The Baptist in Early Christian Tradition," *NTS* 18 (1971), 95-128.
———, "John Did No Miracle: John 10:41," pp. 179-202 in C. F. D. Moule (ed.), *Miracles* (London, 1965).
Barrett, C. K., "John and the Synoptic Gospels," *ET* 85 (1973-74), 228-33.
Becker, J., "Wunder und Christologie," *NTS* 16 (1970), 130-48.
Blinzler, J., *Johannes und die Synoptiker* (Stuttgart, 1965).
Boismard, M.-E. et Lamouille, A., *L'Evangile de Jean* (Paris, 1977), esp. 16-70.
Boismard, M.-E., "Saint Luc et la rédaction du quartrième évangile (Jn 4:46-54)," *RB* 69 (1962), 185-211.
Broome, E. C., "The Sources of the Fourth Gospel," *JBL* 63 (1944), 107-21.
Brown, R. E., *The Gospel According to John,* 2 vols. (Garden City, 1966, 1970), esp. XXVIII-XXXIX.
———, "The Relation of 'The Secret Gospel of Mark' to the Fourth Gospel," *CBQ* 36 (1974), 466-85.
Bultmann, R., *The Gospel of John* (Oxford, 1971).
Cribbs, F. L., "A Study of the Contacts that Exist between St. Luke and St. John," *SBL 1973 Seminar Papers.*
Cullmann, O., *The Johannine Circle* (Philadelphia, 1976).
Dauer, A., *Die Passionsgeschichte im Johannesevangelium: eine traditionsgeschichtliche und theologische Untersuchung zu Joh 18:1–19:30* (Munich, 1972).

Excursus E

Dekker, C., "Grundschrift und Redaction im Johannesevangelium," *NTS* 13 (1966), 66-80.

Dodd, C. H., *Historical Tradition in the Fourth Gospel* (Cambridge, 1963).

Duliere, W. L., *La haute terminologie de la rédaction johannique* (Bruxelles, 1970).

Formesyn, R., *Le sèmeion johannique et le sèmeion hellénistique* (Louvain, 1962).

Fortna, R. T., "Christology in the Fourth Gospel: Redactional-Critical Perspectives," *NTS* 21 (1975), 489-504.

————, "From Christology to Soteriology: A Redaction-Critical Study of Salvation in the Fourth Gospel, *Interpretation* 27 (1973), 31-47.

————, *The Gospel of Signs:* A Reconstruction of the Narrative Source Underlying the Fourth Gospel (Cambridge, 1970).

————, "Source and Redaction in the Fourth Gospel's Portrayal of Jesus' Signs," *JBL* 89 (1970), 51-66.

————, "Theological Use of Locale in the Fourth Gospel," *ATR,* Supplement 3 (1974), 58-94.

Freed, E. D. and Hunt, R. B., "Fortna's Signs-Source in John," *JBL* 94 (1975), 563-79.

Gardner-Smith, P., "St. John's Knowledge of Matthew," *JTS* 4 (1953), 31-35.

Hahn, F., "Der Prozess Jesu nach dem Johannesevangelium," *EKK* 2 (1970), 23-96.

Hartke, W., *Vier urchristliche Parteien und ihre Vereinigung zur apostolischen Kirche* (Berlin, 1961).

Hickling, C. J. A., "Attitudes to Judaism in the Fourth Gospel," M. de Jonge (ed.), *L'Evangile de Jean* (Leuven, 1977), 347-54.

Klein, H., "Die lukanisch-johanneische Passionstradition," *ANW* 67 (1976), 155-86.

Kysar, R., *The Fourth Evangelist and His Gospel* (Minneapolis, 1975), esp. 10-81.

————, "The Source Analysis of the Fourth Gospel, A Growing Consensus?" *NovTest* 15 (1973), 134-52.

Lindars, B., *Behind the Fourth Gospel* (London, 1971).

————, *The Gospel of John* (London, 1972), esp. 25-28, 46-54.

Martyn, J. L., *The Gospel of John in Christian History* (New York, 1979).

————, "Source Criticism and Religionsgeschichte in the Fourth Gospel," *Jesus and Man's Hope (Perspective,* vol. 11, Pittsburgh, 1970), 247-73.

Meeks, W. A., " 'Am I a Jew?'—Johannine Christianity and Judaism," J. Neusner (ed.), *Christianity, Judaism, and Other Greco-Roman Cults* (1975), I, 163-86.

Mender, S., "Zum Problem 'Johannes und die Synoptiker,' " *NTS* 4 (1957-58), 282-307.

Neirynck, F., "John and the Synoptics," M. de Jonge (ed.), *L'Evangile de Jean* (Leuven, 1977), 73-106.

Nicol, W., *The Semeia in the Fourth Gospel* (Leiden, 1972).

Noack, B., *Zur johanneischen Tradition* (Copenhagen, 1954).

Onuki, T., "Die johanneischen Abschiedsreden und die synoptische Tradition," *Annual of the Japanese Biblical Institute* 3 (1977), 157-268.

Parker, P., "Two Editions of John," *JBL* 75 (1956), 303-14.

Perrin, N., *The New Testament, An Introduction* (New York, 1974).

Reim, G., "John IV:44—Crux or Clue?" *NTS* 22 (1976), 476-80.

————, "Probleme der Abschiedsreden," *BZ* 20 (1976), 117-22.

————, *Studien zum alttestamentlichen Hintergrund des Johannesevangeliums*

(Cambridge, 1974).

Richter, G., "Die Gefangennahme Jesu nach dem Johannesevangelium (18:1-12)," *Bibel und Leben* 10 (1969), 26-39.

Robinson, J. M., "The Miracle Source of John," *JAAR* 34 (1971), 339-48.

Robinson, J. M. and Koester, H., *Trajectories Through Early Christianity* (Philadelphia, 1971), 232-68.

Ruckstuhl, E., "Johannine Language and Style. The Question of Their Unity," M. de Jonge (ed.), *L'Evangile de Jean* (Leuven, 1977), 125-48.

———, *Die literarische Einheit des Johannesevangeliums* (Freiburg, 1951).

Sabbe, M., "The Arrest of Jesus in Jn 18, 1-11 and Its Relation to the Synoptic Gospels," M. de Jonge (ed.), *L'Evangile de Jean* (Leuven, 1977), 203-34.

Schnackenburg, R., "Entwicklung und Stand der johanneischen Forchung seit 1955," M. de Jonge (ed.), *L'Evangile de Jean* (Leuven, 1977), 19-44.

———, *The Gospel of St. John* (New York, 1968), esp. 59-74.

———, *Das Johannesevangelium* III Teil (Freiburg, 1975), 463-64.

———, "On the Origin of the Fourth Gospel," *Jesus and Man's Hope* (*Perspective,* vol. 11, Pittsburgh, 1970), 223-46.

Schnider, F. and W. Stenger, *Johannes und die Synoptiker.* Vergleich ihrer Parallelen (Munich, 1971).

Schulz, A., *Das Evangelium nach Johannes* (Göttingen, 1975).

Smith, D. M., *The Composition and Order of the Fourth Gospel:* Bultmann's Literary Theory (New Haven, 1965).

———, "Johannine Christianity: Some Reflections on Its Character and Delineation," *NTS* 21 (1974-75), 229, n. 2.

———, "John 12:12 ff. and the Question of John's Use of the Synoptics," *JBL* 82 (1963), 58-64.

———, "The Setting and Shape of a Johannine Narrative Source," *JBL* 95 (1976), 231-41.

———, "The Sources of the Gospel of John: An Assessment of the present State of the Problem," *NTS* 10 (1963-64), 336-51.

Smith, Morton, *Clement of Alexandria and a Secret Gospel of Mark* (Cambridge, Mass., 1973).

Teeple, H. M., *The Literary Origin of the Gospel of John* (Evanston, 1974).

———, "Methodology in Source Analysis of the Fourth Gospel," *JBL* 81 (1962), 279-86.

Temple, S., *The Core of the Fourth Gospel* (London, 1975).

van Belle, G., *De Sèmeia-bron in het vierde evangelie.* Onstaan en groei van een hypothese (Leuven, 1975).

von Wahlde, U. C., "A Redactional Technique in the Fourth Gospel," *CBQ* 38 (1976), 520-33.

Wilkens, W., *Die Entstehungsgeschichte des vierten Evangeliums* (Zollikon, 1958).

———, "Die Erweckung des Lazarus," *ThZ* (1959), 22-39.

———, *Zeichen und Werke* (Zürich, 1969).

Williams, F., "Fourth Gospel and Synoptic Tradition," *JBL* 86 (1967), 311-19.

Index

169

Index

2. Apocrypha, Pseudepigrapha, Dead Sea Scrolls

172

Index

3. Rabbinic Writings

4. Other Ancient Sources

5. Modern Authors (see also Excursus E)

Index